T0212808

Lecture Notes in Computer Science   8432

Commenced Publication in 1973
Founding and Former Series Editors:
Gerhard Goos, Juris Hartmanis, and Jan van Leeuwen

Editorial Board

David Hutchison
  Lancaster University, Lancaster, UK
Takeo Kanade
  Carnegie Mellon University, Pittsburgh, PA, USA
Josef Kittler
  University of Surrey, Guildford, UK
Jon M. Kleinberg
  Cornell University, Ithaca, NY, USA
Alfred Kobsa
  University of California, Irvine, CA, USA
Friedemann Mattern
  ETH Zürich, Zürich, Switzerland
John C. Mitchell
  Stanford University, Stanford, CA, USA
Moni Naor
  Weizmann Institute of Science, Rehovot, Israel
Oscar Nierstrasz
  University of Bern, Bern, Switzerland
C. Pandu Rangan
  Indian Institute of Technology Madras, Madras, India
Bernhard Steffen
  TU Dortmund University, Dortmund, Germany
Demetri Terzopoulos
  University of California, Los Angeles, CA, USA
Doug Tygar
  University of California, Berkeley, CA, USA
Gerhard Weikum
  Max Planck Institute for Informatics, Saarbrücken, Germany

For further volumes:
http://www.springer.com/series/7409

Tanja E.J. Vos · Kiran Lakhotia
Sebastian Bauersfeld (Eds.)

Future Internet Testing

First International Workshop, FITTEST 2013
Istanbul, Turkey, November 12, 2013
Revised Selected Papers

 Springer

Editors
Tanja E.J. Vos
Sebastian Bauersfeld
Universidad Politécnica de Valencia
Valencia
Spain

Kiran Lakhotia
University College London
London
UK

ISSN 0302-9743   ISSN 1611-3349   (electronic)
ISBN 978-3-319-07784-0   ISBN 978-3-319-07785-7   (eBook)
DOI 10.1007/978-3-319-07785-7
Springer Cham Heidelberg New York Dordrecht London

Library of Congress Control Number: 2014941444

LNCS Sublibrary: SL3 – Information Systems and Applications, incl. Internet/Web, and HCI

© Springer International Publishing Switzerland 2014
This work is subject to copyright. All rights are reserved by the Publisher, whether the whole or part of the material is concerned, specifically the rights of translation, reprinting, reuse of illustrations, recitation, broadcasting, reproduction on microfilms or in any other physical way, and transmission or information storage and retrieval, electronic adaptation, computer software, or by similar or dissimilar methodology now known or hereafter developed. Exempted from this legal reservation are brief excerpts in connection with reviews or scholarly analysis or material supplied specifically for the purpose of being entered and executed on a computer system, for exclusive use by the purchaser of the work. Duplication of this publication or parts thereof is permitted only under the provisions of the Copyright Law of the Publisher's location, in its current version, and permission for use must always be obtained from Springer. Permissions for use may be obtained through RightsLink at the Copyright Clearance Center. Violations are liable to prosecution under the respective Copyright Law.
The use of general descriptive names, registered names, trademarks, service marks, etc. in this publication does not imply, even in the absence of a specific statement, that such names are exempt from the relevant protective laws and regulations and therefore free for general use.
While the advice and information in this book are believed to be true and accurate at the date of publication, neither the authors nor the editors nor the publisher can accept any legal responsibility for any errors or omissions that may be made. The publisher makes no warranty, express or implied, with respect to the material contained herein.

Printed on acid-free paper

Springer is part of Springer Science+Business Media (www.springer.com)

Preface

This volume contains the proceedings of the Future Internet Testing (FITTEST) Workshop, which was held in conjunction with the 25th IFIP International Conference on Testing Software and Systems (ICTSS) in Turkey, Istanbul, in November 2013. The workshop, which was sponsored by the European FP7 Project FITTEST (http://www.pros.upv.es/fittest), was dedicated to advancing the state of the art and practice in verification and testing of future Internet (FI) applications.

The Future Internet Testing Workshop is a dedicated workshop for the software testing community working in the domain of FI applications. Topics included:

- New techniques and tools for testing applications that deal with the dynamic, adaptive, and self-* properties of the future Internet.
- Evaluation of testing tools on real systems through case studies.

The workshop also featured the second round of a competition for Java unit testing tools. This competition was a follow-up on the tool competition run at the Search-Based Software Testing (SBST) workshop held during the International Conference on Software Testing (ICST) in 2013 in Luxembourg. Due to the huge success of this first edition of the competition and the enthusiasm demonstrated by both tool participants and organizers, we decided to run this follow-up at the FITTEST workshop half a year later to see if the tools had improved and were up for a new, bigger, and more difficult benchmark. Moreover, we wanted to continue the stimulating discussions at the workshop about the advantages and disadvantages of particular approaches to the problem. The participants demonstrated their tool at the workshop and presented the results of the competition. The discussion was highly interesting and more competitions are planned.

The Program Committee accepted five regular papers out of eight submissions, whose versions are published in this volume. In addition, the committee included a paper that describes the Java Unit Test Competition held in the context of the workshop as well as a general summary of the achievements of the FITTEST project.

The program chairs would like to thank all of the reviewers for their excellent work and are grateful to the partners involved in the FITTEST project for their support before, during, and after the workshop.

We thank Arthur Baars, Kiran Lakhotia, Peter Kruse, Andrea Arcuri, Gordon Fraser, and Wishnu Prasetya for the work they did in making the tool competition happen.

February 2014

Tanja E.J. Vos
Kiran Lakhotia
Sebastian Bauersfeld

Organization

The Future Internet Testing Workshop was held in the context of the 25th IFIP International Conference on Testing Software and Systems (ICTSS 2013) in November 2013 in Istanbul, Turkey.

Program Chairs

Tanja E.J. Vos   ProS, Universidad Politécnica de Valencia, Spain
Kiran Lakhotia   University College London, UK
Sebastian Bauersfeld   ProS, Universidad Politécnica de Valencia, Spain

Program Committee

Nadia Alshahwan   University of Luxembourg, Luxembourg
Alessandra Bagnato   Softeam, France
Nelly Condori Fernandez   Universidad Politécnica de Valencia, Spain
Mark Harman   University College London, UK
Yue Jia   University College London, UK
Atif Memon   University of Maryland, USA
Bilha Mendelson   IBM Haifa, Israel
John Penix   Google, USA
Justyna Petke   University College London, UK
Andrea Polini   University of Camerino, Italy
Wishnu Prasetya   Universiteit Utrecht, The Netherlands
Simon Poulding   University of York, UK
Scott Tilley   Florida Institute of Technology, USA
Paolo Tonella   Fondazione Bruno Kessler, Italy
Joachim Wegener   Berner & Mattner, Germany

Sponsoring Institutions

EU project Future Internet Testing (FITTEST), contract number 257574
Universidad Politécnica de Valencia, Spain
University College London, UK
Berner & Mattner GmbH, Germany
Fondazione Bruno Kessler, Italy
IBM Israel - Science and Technology LTD IBM, Israel
Universiteit Utrecht, The Netherlands
Softeam, France

Contents

The FITTEST Tool Suite for Testing Future Internet Applications

Tanja E.J. Vos[1]([⊠]), Paolo Tonella[2], I.S. Wishnu B. Prasetya[3],
Peter M. Kruse[4], Onn Shehory[5], Alessandra Bagnato[6], and Mark Harman[7]

[1] Universidad Politécnica de Valencia, Valencia, Spain
`tvos@dsic.upv.es`
[2] Fondazione Bruno Kessler, Trento, Italy
[3] Universiteit van Utrecht, Utrecht, The Netherlands
[4] Berner & Mattner, Berlin, Germany
[5] IBM Research Haifa, Haifa, Israel
[6] Softeam, Paris, France
[7] University College London, London, UK

Abstract. Future Internet applications are expected to be much more
complex and powerful, by exploiting various dynamic capabilities For
testing, this is very challenging, as it means that the range of possible
behavior to test is much larger, and moreover it may at the run time
change quite frequently and significantly with respect to the assumed
behavior tested prior to the release of such an application. The traditional
way of testing will not be able to keep up with such dynamics. The
Future Internet Testing (FITTEST) project (http://crest.cs.ucl.ac.uk/
fittest/), a research project funded by the European Commission (grant
agreement n. 257574) from 2010 till 2013, was set to explore new testing
techniques that will improve our capacity to deal with the challenges
of testing Future Internet applications. Such techniques should not be
seen as replacement of the traditional testing, but rather as a way to
complement it. This paper gives an overview of the set of tools produced
by the FITTEST project, implementing those techniques.

1 Introduction

The Future Internet (FI) will be a complex interconnection of services, applications, content and media running in the cloud. In [1] we describe the main
challenges associated with the testing of applications running in the FI. There
we present a research agenda that has been defined in order to address the
testing challenges identified. The Future Internet Testing (FITTEST) project[1],
a research project funded by the European Commission (grant agreement n.
257574) from 2010 till 2013 to work on part of this research agenda. A whole
range of techniques were developed within the project, which are then implemented as tools; this paper gives an overview of these tools. These tools, and
the kinds of challenges that they can mitigate are listed below.

---

[1] http://crest.cs.ucl.ac.uk/fittest/

T.E.J. Vos, K. Lakhotia, and S. Bauersfeld (Eds.): FITTEST 2013, LNCS 8432, pp. 1–31, 2014.
DOI: 10.1007/978-3-319-07785-7_1, © Springer International Publishing Switzerland 2014

Dynamism and self-adaptation. The range of behaviours of an FI application with such properties is very hard to predict in advance. We propose to complement traditional testing with *continuous testing* where the testwares are evolved together with the application. We have a set of tools to support this. These tools automatically infer behavioural models and oracles from monitored executions and uses these models to automate test case generation. This can be run in cycles and unattended, between the traditional pre-release testing rounds.

Large scale and rapid evolution of components. To meet rapid technology and business changes, components of FI applications will have to evolve even quicker than what now already is. Each time we integrate components, we face a critical decision of either to use the new components, or to simply stay with the old ones, knowing that they might have issues, risks, and limited support. Unfortunately, more often than not, the latter is the preferred choice since the incurred regression testing activities are too time consuming since there are too many tests. We therefore propose to *prioritize* the tests, according to the available time and budget. The FITTEST regression testing approach aims at automatically prioritizing a set of test cases based on their sensitivity to external changes. The key idea is to give priority to the tests that can detect a high number of artificial changes.

Large Feature-configuration Space. FI applications will be highly customisable; it offers a whole range of features that can be configured, as well as configurations that depend on the user's context and environment. As the result, the space of possible configurations is combinatorially large. To deal with this, we developed and/or improved three different approaches for combinatorial testing: (1) The CTE XL Professional by Berner & Mattner is a context-sensitive graphical editor and a very powerful tool for the systematic specification and design of test cases using a combinatorial approach based on Classification Trees; (2) The IBM Focus tool is a comprehensive tool for test-oriented system modelling, for model based test planning, and for functional coverage analysis. Its system modelling and test planning are based on computing Cartesian products of system or test aspects, with restrictions applied to the models and henceforth to the computation; (3) The Hyper Heuristic Search Algorithm that uses a hyperheuristic search based algorithm to generate test data. Hyperheuristics are a new class of Search Based Software Engineering algorithms, the members of which use dynamic adaptive optimisation to learn optimisation strategies without supervision.

Low observability. FI applications have low observability: their underlying internal states are complex, but we are limited in how we can inspect them. This makes it problematical for a test case to infer that an application has done something incorrect. However, quite often an incorrect state, when interacted on, can eventually trigger an observable failure, enabling us to at least observe that something has gone wrong. Our *rogue user testing* tool is a fully automatic testing framework, that tests FI applications at the GUI level. It uses the operating systems Accessibility API to recognize GUI controls and their properties and enables programmatic interaction with them. It derives sets of possible actions for each state that the GUI is in and automatically selects and executes appropriate ones in order to drive the GUI and eventually crash it. After starting the target application, it proceeds to scan the GUI in order to obtain the state of all control elements on the screen from which it generates a hierarchical representation called a widget tree. This tree enables it to derive a set of sensible actions. According to the Rogue User's internal search state, it now selects promising actions and executes these to test the system with rogue user behaviour.

Asynchronous, time and load dependent behaviour. Testing the concurrent part of an application is made difficult by dependency on factors like communication noise, delays, message timings, and load conditions. The resulting behavior is highly non-deterministic. Errors that only happen under specific schedules are very difficult to trigger. We have enhanced IBM's Concurrency Testing tool (ConTest), which is based on the idea of selectively inserting noises in the application to increase the likelihood to trigger concurrency errors.

Sections 2–6 will describe these tools; they can be downloaded from FITTEST software site[2]. Effort has also been taken to evaluate the tools against a number of industrial case studies. These case studies are listed in Sect. 7, with references to the papers or reports that describe the studies in more details.

2 Continuous Testing

We envisage FI applications to be much more dynamic. They are capable of self-modifications, context and environment dependent autonomous behaviours, as well as allowing user defined customisation and dynamic re-configurations. Services and components could be dynamically added by customers and the intended use could change significantly. Moreover, these self-adaption and dynamic changes can be expected to happen frequently while the application is alive. The range of possible classes of behavior is thus much larger; and it is just very hard to anticipate them all during the testing, which traditionally happens before we release the software. The resulting traditional testwares might thus be already inadequate for a specific executing instance of the system.

Indeed, some parts of such applications may remain fairly static, so traditional testing will still play an important part in the overall testing of an FI application. But the testwares of the dynamic parts of the application will need to evolve together with the system: new test cases may need to be added, some to be removed, and some to be adapted to the changed functionalities. We therefore propose to complement traditional testing with continuous testing.

Continuous testing is carried out in cycles, throughout the lifetime of the current release of the System Under Test (SUT), until at least its next release. Each cycle consists of the activities shown in Fig. 1. Before the SUT is deployed, a logger is first attached to it; if necessary by instrumenting the

---

[2] https://code.google.com/p/fittest

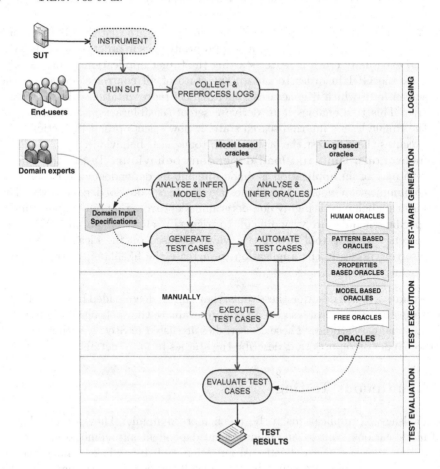

Fig. 1. Activities performed in each testing cycle

SUT. Logs are then collected and then analyzed to infer a behavior model of the SUT, in the form of a finite state machine, as well as properties to be used as test oracles. Fresh logs from the current cycle are used for this analysis, but also logs from previous cycles up to some time in the past, which we consider to still represent the current SUT. Test cases are then generated from the model by traversing it according to proper criteria, such as transition coverage. Each test case is basically a path of transitions through the finite state machine. Since self adaptation or other forms of dynamic changes will be visible on the logs, the inferred model can keep up with them. However, using a model inferred like this to test the SUT is only meaningful if the generated test cases do not simply replay the logged executions. We therefore apply e.g. a combinatoric approach over the parameters of the execution in order to trigger fresh executions. Test cases generated from a model are typically still abstract. They are then refined to concrete test cases and then executed. Since the used test oracles are also inferred from logs, they are not guaranteed to be sound nor complete. Therefore, violations reported also need to be inspected to check if they really represent errors. After all errors are fixed, the current cycle ends. After some period of time, or if we have a reason to believe that the SUT has changed, the next cycle is started. Importantly, every cycle is mostly automatic (and it is, except for the errors analysis and bugs fixing part). Such a log-based approach may not be as strong as it would be if we have the ground truth (which we don't), but at least now we do not leave the dynamic parts of the SUT completely untested.

In FITTEST we have developed a set of tools to support the activities in Fig. 1. Most of these tools are integrated in an Integrated Testing Environment (ITE). This ITE is a distributed test environment, with the main component, in charge of model/oracle inference and test case generation, running at the tester's workstation. Through remote agents it monitors and collects data from the SUT running in its production environment. The SUT may in turn consist of a server part and users' clients, running the application within a Web browser. ITE's agents are deployed to monitor them. The inference of models from logs can be done from the ITE, as well as the generation and execution of test cases. The inference and checking of oracles use separate tools. To execute the generated test-cases the ITE can also control a version of the SUT that runs in a dedicated testing environment. Tools and libraries for logging and test case execution depend on the technologies used by the SUT. Currently the ITE supports PHP and Flash applications.

2.1 Logging and Instrumentation

Loggers intercept events representing top level interactions with the application under test (this way programmers do not need to explicitly write any logging code). The used technology determines what constitutes a top level interaction. For a PHP application, top level interactions are the HTTP requests sent by the client to the application. For a Flash application, these are GUI events, such as the user filling a textfield or clicking on a button. The produced logs are in the text-based FITTEST format [2]. The format is compact, but deeply structured, allowing deep object serialization into the logs. In the Flash logger, we can register serialization delegates. They specify how instances of the classes they delegate are to be serialized. Using such a delegate one can also specify an abstract projection of the application's concrete state and log it. Although the delegates have to be manually specified, they are 'transparent' (the application is not even aware them).

The PHP logger does not currently log state information, hence models inferred from PHP logs are purely event-based. For Flash, the ITE also includes a bytecode instrumentation tool called *abci* [3], to instrument selected methods and instruction-blocks for logging, thus allowing much more detailed logs to be produced. Abci is implemented with the AG attribute grammar framework [4], allowing future extensions, such as adding more instrumentation types, to be programmed more abstractly.

2.2   Model Inference

Model inference is a key activity in continuous testing [5,6]. Based on execution traces, it infers models that describe structure and behaviour of a SUT using either event-sequence abstraction or state abstraction [7–9]. One of the most frequently used models is the Finite State Machine (FSM). In an FSM, nodes represent states of the SUT, and transitions represent an application event/action (e.g., a method call, an event handler) that can change the application state, if executed. Additionally, guards and conditions can enrich the model to capture the context in which events and actions are executed.

In the ITE, models are automatically inferred from logs using either event-sequence abstraction or state abstraction. The outcome are FSM models that can be fed to the successive phases of the ITE cycle (specifically, event sequence generation and input data generation). Models are updated continuously and incrementally [10] as the software evolves and new behaviours appear in the execution logs.

The events in the model often have input parameters. From the log we extract concrete input values for such parameters. We have implemented a data mining technique to infer input classes (for combinatorial testing, used later in test generation) for these parameters [11].

2.3   Oracle Inference

The tool Haslog and Lopi are used to infer oracles from logs. Hashlog can infer pre- and post-conditions for each type of high level event; it uses Daikon [12] at the back-end. In Fig. 1 these are called *properties based oracles*. If the logged (abstract) state consists of many variables, simply passing them all to Daikon will cause Daikon to try to infer all sorts of relations between them, most of which are actually not interesting for us. The ITE allows groups of variables to be specified (using regular expressions) and constrains Daikon to only infer the oracles for each group separately.

Lopi infers so-called *pattern-based oracles* [13]. These are algebraic equations of common patterns over high level events, e.g. $a = \epsilon$ or $bb = b$, saying that on any state, executing the event b twice will lead to the same state as executing just one b. Additionally, such equations are also useful to reduce a failing log (log produced by a failing execution) when we diagnose the failure [14].

Finally, through instrumentation we can also log the entry and exit points of selected methods, allowing pre- and post-conditions to be inferred for them. Furthermore, so-called *sub-cases* oracles can also be inferred [15]. This requires "instructions blocks" to be instrumented as well—for each method, transitions between these blocks form the method's control flow graph. Visit patterns over these blocks can be specified and used as a form of *splitters* [16], yielding stronger oracles.

2.4   Test Case Generation

Two methods for input data generation are available: classification trees and search-based input generation. Classification trees require one additional input: a partitioning of the possible inputs into equivalence classes, represented as classification trees. When such classification trees are available, the tool combines event sequence generation with pairwise coverage criteria to produce concrete, executable test cases (combinatorial-model-based test generation). The search-based input data generation method can be used when classification trees are unavailable or as a complementary method with respect to classification trees. It uses evolutionary, search-based testing, to automatically produce concrete test cases (including input values), which achieve transition coverage of the model inferred through dynamic model inference.

Combinatorial-Model-Based Test Generation. This method [17] starts from a finite state model and applies model-based testing to generate test paths that represent sequences of events to be executed against the SUT. Several algorithms are used to generate test paths, ranging from simple graph visit algorithms, to advanced techniques based on maximum diversity of the event frequencies, and semantic interactions between successive events in the sequence.

Such paths are, then, transformed to classification trees using the CTE XL[3] format, enriched with domain input classifications such as data types and partitions. Then, test combinations are generated from those trees using t-way combinatorial criteria. Finally, they are transformed to an executable format depending on the target application (e.g., using Selenium[4]). Note that although these test cases are generated from models learned from the SUT's own behaviour, the combinatorial stage will trigger fresh behaviour, thus testing the SUT against the learned patterns.

Thanks to the integration with CTE XL, other advanced analysis can be performed on the classification trees. For example, we can impose dependencies on the input classifications and filter the test combinations that violate the dependencies to remove invalid tests.

Search-Model-Based Test Generation. In this approach [18] the ITE transforms the inferred models and the conditions that characterize the states of the models into a Java program. It then uses evolutionary, search-based testing, to automatically produce test cases that achieve branch coverage on the Java representation. Specifically, we use Evosuite [19] for this task. Branch coverage solved by Evosuite has been theoretically shown to be equivalent to transition coverage in the original models. Finally, the test cases generated by Evosuite require a straightforward transformation to be usable to test our SUT.

---

[3] http://www.cte-xl-professional.com
[4] http://seleniumhq.org

2.5   Test Evaluation

The generated test-cases are executed and checked against oracles. If an oracle is violated, the corresponding test case has then failed, Further investigation is needed to understand the reason behind the failure. Support for automatic debugging is currently beyond our scope. As depicted in Fig. 1, various oracles can be used for test evaluation. The most basic and inexpensive oracles detect SUT crashes; the most effective but expensive are human oracles. The ITE offers several other types of oracles that are automatically inferred from the logs or the models.

Model-Based Oracles. The test cases produced by the ITE are essentially paths generated from the FSM models. If these models can be validated as not too much under-approximating, then any path through them can be expected to be executable: it should not the SUT to crash or become stuck in the middle, which can be easily checked. In Fig. 1 this is called *model-based oracles*.

Properties- and Pattern-Based Oracles. The executions of the test cases are also logged. The ITE then analyzes the produced logs to detect violations to the inferred pre- and post-conditions as well as the pattern-based oracles. The checking of the latter is done at the suite level rather than at the test case level. E.g. to check $bb = b$ the ITE essentially looks for a pair of prefix sequences σbb and σb in the logs produced by the test suite that contradicts the equation.

3   Regression Testing

Audit testing of services is a form of regression testing [20, 21] that aims at checking the compliance of a new service, including a new version of an existing service or a newly-discovered service from a new provider, with a FI System Under Test (SUT) that integrates the service and currently works properly. In such a context, test case prioritization has the goal of giving an order to the test cases, so that the key ones (e.g., those that reveal faults) are executed earlier.

Audit testing of services differs from traditional regression testing because the testing budget is typically much more limited (only a very small subset of the regression test suite can be executed) and because the kind of changes that are expected in the service composition is known and quite specific. In fact, audit testing is used to check the proper functioning of a service composition when some external services change. Some adaptations of the service composition that are required to make the composition work are trivially detected at the syntactical level, by the compiler which will immediately report any interface change that needs adaptation on the composition side. It is only those semantic changes that do not affect the service API description (for example WSDL [22]) that may go undetected and require audit testing. The FITTEST approach to test case prioritization for audit testing of services, called *Change Sensitivity Test Prioritization* (CSTP), is based on the idea that the most important test cases are those that can detect mutations of the service responses, when such mutations affect the semantics, while leaving the WSDL syntax unchanged. More details about CSTP, including its empirical validation, are available in a previous publication [23].

Let s be the service under consideration, s_{new} be a candidate that can substitute s. s_{new} is the subject of audit testing. Let TS be the set of available test cases that are selected as candidate for audit testing. These are the test cases whose executions result in the invocation of s. TS is used in audit testing of s_{new} with respect to the composition under consideration. In practice, execution of the full suite TS might involve too much time or might require a big monetary budget, if only a limited number of invocations of s_{new} is available for testing purposes (i.e., invocations in test mode) or if the invocation of s_{new} requires payment. Hence, the service integrator has to minimize and prioritize the test cases from TS that are actually run against s_{new} during audit testing. The goal is then to prioritize the test cases in such a way that issues, if any, are detected by an initial small subset of the ranked test cases.

CSTP determines the *change sensitivity* of the test cases and uses this metrics to rank the test cases, from the most sensitive to service changes to the least sensitive one. Change sensitivity measures how sensitive a test case is to changes occurring to the service under consideration. The rationale underlying this approach is that new versions of services may produce service responses that are still compliant with the service interface (WSDL), but violate some assumptions made (often implicitly) by the service integrator when building the service composition. Thus, test cases that are more sensitive to these changes are executed first.

Specifically, we have defined a set of new mutation operators and we apply them to the service responses to inject artificial changes. Our mutation operators are based on a survey of implicit assumptions commonly made on Web service responses and on manual inspection of those parts of the service API which is described only informally (usually by comments inside the WSDL document). After applying our mutations, we measure change sensitivity for each test case by comparing the outputs of each test case in two situations: with the original response, and with the mutated responses. A change is detected if the behaviour of the service composition differs when the original service is used as compared to the mutated response. Similarly to the mutation score, the change sensitivity score is the number of changes detected (mutants killed) over all changes.

The measuring of change sensitivity is divided into six steps (see Fig. 2): (1) executing the SUT on the regression test suite TS; (2) monitoring the service requests and collecting the response messages; (3) generating mutated responses by means of mutation operators, based on service assumptions; (4) for each test case, running the SUT and comparing the behaviour of the SUT when receiving the original response and when the mutated ones are received. Then, (5) the sensitivity (mutation) score is calculated and (6) test cases are ranked by mutation score.

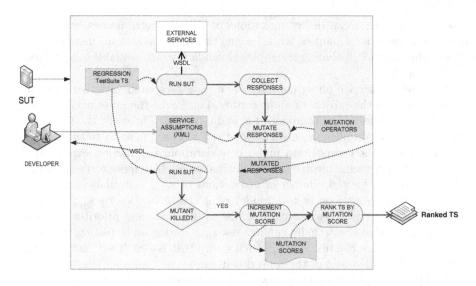

Fig. 2. Activities performed when applying CSTP

3.1   Change Sensitivity Measure

In the context of Webservices, service clients communicate with services via message passing: clients send requests to services and receive responses. During an audit testing session at the client side, test inputs are provided to the client system, which, then, sends requests to services, and receives and processes the responses. Finally, the outputs from the system are evaluated (the test oracle takes usually the form of assertions, the default assertions being that the application should not crash or raise exceptions). Since the client lacks controllability and observability over the service, and SLA (Service Level Agreement) [24] concerns only high-level quality contracts (e.g. performance, response time), the developer of the client (service integrator) has to make assumptions about technical details regarding the format of the responses. We call these assumptions as *service integrator's assumptions*. For example, the integrator might expect a list of phone numbers, separated by commas, from the service, when searching for a phone number. Changes in the data format of the response (e.g., using colon instead of comma as phone number separator) may break the assumptions of the service integrator, which may lead the client to misbehave, thus making the test cases not to pass.

It is worth noticing that we focus on data changes (e.g. format, range, etc.). Changes regarding the structure of the service responses can be easily detected, because they require the interface definition of the service, written for instance in the Web Service Definition Language (WSDL) [22], to be changed. Adopting a new service interface involves rebinding and recompiling, and the compiler is able to detect syntactic incompatibilities. What the compiler cannot detect is (subtle) semantic incompatibilities (such as the change of a list item separator). This requires regression (audit) testing and test prioritization.

In CSTP, service integrators specify their service assumptions explicitly, in order to simplify and automate audit testing of integrated services. For the specification of the integrator's assumptions, we propose an XML based assumption specification language. A service assumption consists of an XPath reference [25] to an element in the response under consideration and it can include data restrictions regarding that element. Data restrictions have the same format as those defined in the W3C XML Schema [26]. Service assumptions specify what a client expects from a service for its own purposes. Therefore, the data restrictions specified by one service integrator may differ from those in the service definition (e.g. in the WSDL interface of the service) or from those specified by another integrator.

The mutation operators that we propose use service assumptions to inject artificial changes into service responses. The changed responses (also called mutated responses) and the original ones are, then, used to measure change sensitivity of test cases. In the following sections we discuss mutation operators and how change sensitivity is measured.

3.2 Mutation Operators

Based on a survey of service assumptions commonly made on Web service responses and on manual inspection of those parts of the service interface which is described only informally, usually by annotations or comments inside the WSDL document, we identified 9 main data restriction types and their corresponding mutation operators, showed in Table 1.

The *Enumeration* mutation operator randomly generates a new item, added to the finite set of items admitted in the response according to the service assumption. The *Length* mutation operator changes the size of a response element, so as to make it differ from the integrator's assumptions. Similarly, the *MaxLength* and *MinLength* mutation operators make the size of a response element respectively greater than or lower than the limit admitted in the integrator's assumptions. When the numeric value of a response element is constrained to be within boundaries, the *MinInclusive, MaxInclusive, MinExclusive, MaxExclusive* mutation operators produce values that lie beyond the integrator's assumed boundaries. The *RegEx* mutation operators can be used when the content of a response element is supposed to follow a pattern specified by means of a regular expression. Such regular expression is mutated (e.g., by replacing a constant character with a different one; by making a mandatory part of the expression optional; by concatenating an additional subexpression) and mutated responses are generated by means of the mutated regular expression. For example, the regular expression specifying a list of phone numbers as a list of comma separated digit sequences can be mutated by replacing the constant character ',' with ':'.

Taking a data restriction specified in a service assumption as an input, the corresponding mutation operator can generate new data that are not acceptable

Table 1. Mutation operators to inject changes in service responses

Operator	Description
Enumeration	Enumeration restriction limits the content of an XML element to a set of acceptable values. Using this restriction *Enumeration* operator generates a new value which is not accepted by the restriction to replace the original one
Length	Length restriction limits the precise length of the content of an XML element. Using this restriction *Length* operator generates a new content having its length differs from the required one
MaxLength	Length restriction limits the length of the content of an XML element to be inferior than a specific value. Using this restriction *MaxLength* operator generates a new content having its length greater than the allowed one
MinLength	Length restriction requires the length of the content of an XML element to be greater than a specific value. Using this restriction *MinLength* operator generates a new content having its length smaller than the allowed one
MinInclusive, MaxInclusive, MinExclusive, MaxExclusive	These restrictions are specified on numeric types, e.g. double, integer. The corresponding mutation operators generate new numeric numbers that are smaller or greater than the acceptable minimum or maximum values
RegEx	Regular expression restriction requires the content of an XML element to follow a specific pattern. *RegEx* based operators change slightly the original regular expression and generates new values based on the mutated expression. CSTP implements six *RegEx* based operators [23]

according to the service assumption. This is to simulate the fact that when we plan to substitute s with s_{new}, s_{new} may have data that violate the current service integrator's assumptions.

3.3 Measuring Change Sensitivity

Let us assume that the original responses are monitored and collected locally (see Fig. 2); at the next step, we apply the mutation operators discussed in previous section (based on the service integrator's assumption specifications) to generate mutated responses. For each response and for each assumption, we select a mutation operator based on the type of restriction specified. The XPath is used to query the elements in the response to be injected with new contents generated by the mutation operator. Eventually, we obtain a set of N mutated responses, each of them containing one change.

Then, each test case in the regression test suite is executed offline against the N mutated responses. Instead of querying s to get the response, the system receives a mutated response and processes it. In this way we can conduct test prioritization without any extra cost for accessing s, if applicable, and without any time delay, due to the network connection with external services. The behaviour of the system reacting to the mutated responses is compared to its behaviour with the original response. Any deviation observed (i.e., different outputs, assertions violated, crash or runtime exceptions reported) implies the change is detected (or the mutant is killed). Change sensitivity of a test case is measured as the proportion of mutants that are killed by each test case.

The change sensitivity metrics is then used to prioritize the test cases. Only those at higher priority will be run against the real, external services, during online audit testing. The monetary and execution costs associated with such kind of testing make it extremely important to prioritize the test cases, such that the top ranked ones are also the most important, in terms of capability of revealing actual problems due to service changes that are not managed at the purely syntactic level. We conducted a case study to assess the effectiveness of our prioritization method in terms of fault revealing capability, under the assumption that the resources for online audit testing are extremely scarce, hence the fault revealing test cases should be ranked very high in the prioritized list produced by our method, in order for them to have a chance of being actually executed during real audit testing. Results show that using only a subset of around 10 % of the available test cases (those top-ranked by our approach), most injected faults can be detected [23]. Moreover, CSTP outperformed coverage-based test case prioritization.

4   Combinatorial Testing

Combinatorial testing, also called combinatorial interaction testing [27] or combinatorial test design, is a technique that designs tests for a system under test by combining input parameters. For each parameter of the system, a value is chosen. This collection of parameter values is called test case. The set of all test cases constitutes the test suite for the system under test. Combinatorial testing can be a good approach to achieve software quality. The t-wise combination is a good compromise between effort of testing and fault detection rate [28].

The most common coverage criterion is 2-wise (or *pairwise*) testing, that is fulfilled if all possible pairs of values are covered by at least one test case in the result test set.

4.1   The Classification Tree Method

The classification tree method [29] offers a well studied approach for combinatorial testing. Applying the classification tree method involves two steps—designing the classification tree and defining test cases.

Designing the Classification Tree. In the first phase, all aspects of interests and their disjoint values are identified. Aspects of interests, also known as parameters, are called *classifications*, their corresponding parameter values are called *classes*.

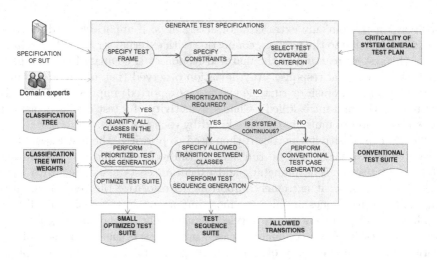

Fig. 3. The CTE workflow

Each classification can have any number of disjoint classes, describing the occurrence of the parameter. All classifications together form the *classification tree*. For semantic purpose, classifications can be grouped into *compositions*. Additionally, all classes can be refined using new classifications with classes again. In Fig. 3 this activity is called Specification of Test Frame and to be found in the upper part. Afterwards, the specification of constraints (or dependency rules as they are called in the classification tree method) [30] follows.

Definition of Test Cases. Having composed the classification tree, test cases are defined by combining classes of different classifications. For each classification, a significant representative (class) is selected. Classifications and classes of classifications are disjoint.

The Classification Tree Editor (CTE) is a graphical editor to create and maintain classification trees [31]. During the FITTEST project the CTE XL Professional by Berner & Mattner has received substantial improvement.

Started as a graphical editor [32] for combinatorial test design [33], the tool now features the following leading edge functionalities: Prioritized test case generation using weights in the classification tree on the combinatorial aspects allows automatically generating test suites ordered by the importance of each test case, easing the selection of valuable subsets [34, 35] (lower left part of Fig. 3). Important classes (or class tuples) are combined into early test cases while less important classes (or tuples) are used later in the resulting test suite. The prioritization allows the tester to optimize a test suite by selecting subsets and, therefore, to reduce test efforts. The weights can also be used for statistical testing (e.g. in fatigue test).

The other new generation technique goes beyond conventional functional black-box testing by considering the succession of individual test steps. The automated generation of test sequences uses a multi-agent system to trigger the system under test with input values in a meaningful order, so that all possible system states are reached [36] (as seen in the bottom center part of Fig. 3).

Coverage criteria for both generation techniques are also available. New mechanisms for describing numerical dependencies [30] have been established as well as part of the FITTEST project. For all generation techniques available, the use of search based techniques [37] has been considered as part of controlled benchmarks [38].

4.2   Focus CTD

The IBM Focus tool is a comprehensive tool for test-oriented system modeling, for model based test planning, and for functional coverage analysis. Its system modeling and test planning are based on computing Cartesian products of system or test aspects, with restrictions applied to the models and henceforth to the computation. The generated test plans are combinatorial, thus placing the IBM Focus tool in the family of combinatorial test design tools [32,39], including CTE.

The Focus tool also provides advanced code coverage analysis capabilities. It imports code coverage data from other tools and analyzes various coverage aspects. In particular it excels in identifying system parts which are poorly covered, and in planning tests to optimally cover those system parts.

Focus provides advanced reports, independent of the programming language and the platform. The Focus graphical user interface (GUI) allows manual activation, viewing and manipulation of its modeling and combinatorial test design capabilities and of its coverage analysis. Additionally, the GUI can be bypassed to facilitate automatic or semi-automatic test planning and coverage analysis. The results of the tool and its reports can be exported into HTML, spreadsheet, and text files.

The main functionality of the Focus tool is depicted in Fig. 4. Given a system under test (SUT), system attributes and attribute values are extracted. Additionally, restrictions are placed on the attributes, their values, and the dependencies among them. Based on these, a combinatorial model of the system is generated by Focus. Focus may be stopped at this stage, however the common usage proceeds to test plan generation. The tool can generate a plan from scratch, or alternatively start from an existing plan. Either way, the plan is optimized to meet coverage, cost and functional requirements. Manual changes are allowed via the GUI, supporting "what-if" style modifications. Once the test plan is optimized and meets user requirements, Focus can automatically generate the needed test cases.

4.3   Hyperheuristic Search Algorithm

Much research in the literature of combinatorial testing has been focused on the development of bespoke algorithms tailored for specific combinatorial problems. For example, some algorithms have been designed for solving unconstrained

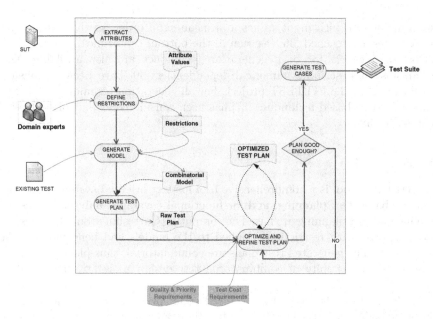

Fig. 4. Focus' flow

problems [40–43], while others have been tuned for constrained interaction problems [44, 45]. This leaves tester many different algorithms which have very different properties. Problem occurs when testers are not familiar with these techniques, because an algorithm designed for one type of combinatorial problem may perform poorly when applied to another.

To address this problem we introduce a simulated annealing hyperheuristic search based algorithm [46]. Hyperheuristics are a new class of Search Based Software Engineering algorithms, the members of which use dynamic adaptive optimisation to learn optimisation strategies without supervision [47, 48]. Our hyperheuristic algorithm learns the combinatorial strategy to apply dynamically, as it is executed. This single algorithm can be applied to a wide range of combinatorial problem instances, regardless of their structure and characteristics.

There are two subclasses of hyperheuristic algorithms: generative and selective [48]. Generative hyperheuristics combine low level heuristics to generate new higher level heuristics. Selective hyperheuristics select from a set of low level heuristics. In our work, we use a selective hyperheuristic algorithm. Selective hyperheuristic algorithms can be further divided into two classes, depending upon whether they are online or offline. We use online selective hyperheuristics, since we want a solution that can learn to select the best combinatorial heuristic to apply, unsupervised, as it executes.

The overall workflow of our hyperheuristic algorithm is depicted in Fig. 5. The algorithm takes a combinatorial model generated from system under test as a input. It outputs a covering array model which can be converted to a test suite with the help of domain experts. The hyperheuristic algorithm contains a set of

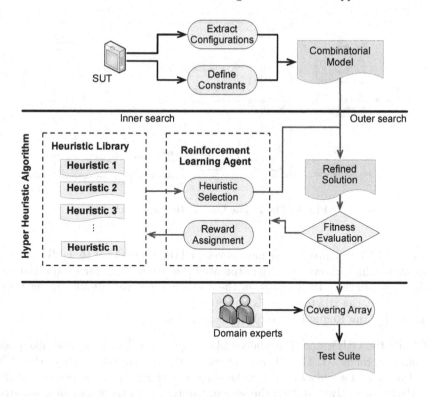

Fig. 5. The hyperheuristic search algorithm workflow

lower level heuristics and two layer of heuristic search. The first (or outer) layer
uses a normal metaheuristic search to find solutions directly from the solution
space of the problem. The inner layer heuristic, searches for the best candidate
lower heuristics for the outer layer heuristics in the current problem state. As
a result, the inner search adaptively identifies and exploits different strategies
according to the characteristics of the problems it faces. A full explanation and
evaluation of the algorithm can be found in our technical report [46].

5   Rogue User Testing

Graphical User Interfaces (GUIs) represent the main connection point between a
software's components and its end users and can be found in almost all modern
applications. Vendors strive to build more intuitive and efficient interfaces to
guarantee a better user experience, making them more powerful but at the same
time much more complex. Especially since the rise of smartphones and tablets,
this complexity has reached a new level and threatens the efficient testability
of applications at the GUI level. To cope with this challenge, it is necessary to
automate the testing process and simulate the rogue user.

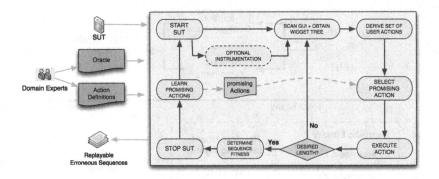

Fig. 6. The Rogue User testing approach

In the FITTEST project, we have developed the Rogue User tool (RU), a Java application which allows to write automated robustness tests for FI applications at the User Interface level and from the user's perspective [49,50]. In Fig. 6 the approach that the RU tool uses is depicted.

Basically, the Rogue User tool works as follows:

1. Obtain the GUI's state (i.e. the visible widgets and their properties like position, size, focus ...). The RU can determine the current GUI state of the SUT in the form of a *widget tree*. A widget tree is a hierarchical composition of the widgets currently visible on the screen, together with the values of associated widget attributes. Figure 7 shows an example of such a tree for some user interface.
2. Derive a set of sensible default actions: Enabled buttons, icons and hyperlinks can be tapped, text fields can be tapped and filled with text, the screen, scrollbars and sliders may be dragged, etc. RU allows to simulate simple (clicks, keystrokes) as well as complex actions (drag and drop operations, handwriting and other gestures, etc.) and can thus drive even sophisticated GUIs.
3. Select and execute an action.
4. Apply an oracle to check whether the state is valid. If it is invalid, stop sequence generation and save the suspicious sequence to a dedicated directory, for later replay.
5. If a determined given amount of sequences has been generated, stop sequence generation, else go to step 1.

The tool offers the user a simple user interface (see Fig. 8), there are mainly four buttons, which start the RU into its four main modes:

1. Start in Spy-Mode: This mode does not execute any actions. It will start the System under Test (SUT) and allows you to inspect the GUI. Simply use the mouse cursor to point on a widget and the Rogue User will display everything it knows about it. The Spy-Mode will also visualize the set of actions that

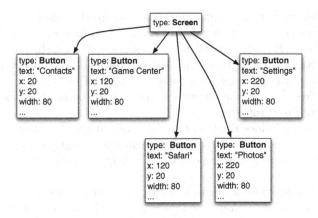

Fig. 7. Widget tree

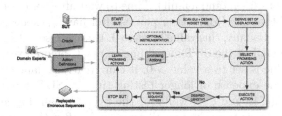

Fig. 8. The Rogue User testing tools simple interface

the Rogue User recognizes, so that you can see which ones will be executed during a test.

2. Start in Generation-Mode: This mode will start the SUT and execute a full test on the SUT.
3. Start in Replay-Mode: This mode replays a previously recorded sequence. The Rogue User will ask you for the sequence to replay.
4. Start in View-Mode: The View-Mode allows you to inspect all steps of a pre-viously recorded sequence. Contrary to the Replay-Mode, it will not execute any actions, but only show you the screenshots that were recorded during sequence generation. This is ideal if a sequence turns out not to be repro-ducible.

Then there are various tabs that allow the tester to configure the tool. The *general settings* tab enables the tester to specify where the SUT is, how many sequences to generate, the maximum length of the sequences, etc.

The *Oracle* tab helps in specifying simple oracles based on the state of the GUI of the SUT. For example, we can enter a regular expression that describes those messages that you consider to be related to possible errors. The RU will apply this expression to each title of each widget on the screen. If it matches any widgets title, the RU will report an error and save the sequence for later inspection. Moreover, this tab allows us to configure the "freeze time". The RU is able to detect crashes automatically, because it realizes when the SUT is not running anymore. However, if the SUT does not really crash, but just freezes (is unresponsive) for a long time, then the RU does not know whether it is just carrying out heavy computations or hangs. If the SUT is unresponsive for more than the set freeze time, the RU will consider it to be crashed and mark the current sequence as erroneous.

The *filter* tab provides the tester an easy way to specify actions that should not be executed (e.g. because they are undesirable or dangerous), or processes that can be killed during test generation (i.e. help windows, document viewers, etc.).

The *time* tab provides a means to define: Action Duration (The higher this value, the longer the execution of actions will take. Mouse movements and typing become slower, so that it is easier to follow what the Rogue User is doing. This can be useful during Replay-Mode, in order to replay a recorded sequence with less speed to better understand a fault); Time to wait after execution of an action (This is the time that the Rogue User pauses after having executed an action in Generation-Mode. Usually, this value is set to 0. However, sometimes it can make sense to give the GUI of the SUT more time to react, before executing the next action. If this value is set to a value > 0, it can greatly enhance reproducibility of sequences at the expense of longer testing times.); SUT startup time (This is the time that the Rogue User waits for the SUT to load. Large and complex SUTs might need more time than small ones. Only after this time has expired, the Rogue User will start sequence generation.); Maximum test time in seconds (The RU will cease to generate any sequences after this time has elapsed. This is useful for specifying a test time out, e.g. 1 h, one day, one week.); Use Recorded Action Timing during Replay (This option only affects Replay-Mode. If checked, the RU will use the action duration and action wait time that was used during sequence generation. If you uncheck the option, you can specify your own values).

6   Concurrency Testing

Many concurrency bugs originate from the need for shared resources, e.g., local memory for multi-threaded applications or network storage for FI applications. Shared memory requires access protection. Inadequate protection results in data corruption or invalid data reads (races). The protection mechanisms themselves can lead to further bugs, notably deadlocks. Other bugs result from broken assumptions about order of actions, or about completion time of actions.

The IBM Concurrency Testing tool (ConTest in short) facilitates various aspects of handling concurrency bugs of FI applications and is capable of identifying concurrency bugs [51]. We have improved this tool. We have extended ConTest with a number of new capabilities. Whereas before it works on monolithic software, it is now significantly extended to support the special concurrency testing and debugging needs of internet-based applications. Such applications are typically distributed, componentized, interact in high level protocols (such as http), and in

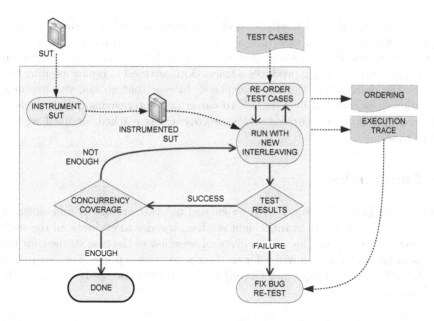

Fig. 9. The ConTest flow

times are composed in an ad hoc manner. The main idea is that concurrency bugs, either local ones or distributed across an internet-wide system, can be expressed in terms of event or message ordering. Changes in the ordering of messages and events can expose bugs which are otherwise dormant. This is exactly what ConTest does to expose concurrency bugs. While executing the application with multiple orderings can expose bugs, it does not isolate them. Within FITTEST, ConTest was enhanced with bug isolation capabilities, which allows learning which component or components of the system contain the bug. This is of paramount importance in internat applications, which are componentized and distributed.

Another FITTEST addition to ConTest is a high-level record-and-replay capability, which enables debugging the "suspicious" component in isolation while maintaining the communication patterns that manifest the bug. This, again, is very important in internet applications where communication is commonly central to the system, yet there is a need to debug specific components in isolation.

Yet another FITTEST extension to ConTest is an orange box facility. The orange box allows replay of the series of messages and events which took place just ahead of a concurrency bug manifestation. This provide much help to concurrency debugging of FI applications. Deadlock analysis and lock history were also added to the FITTEST version of ConTest to further improve concurrency testing and debugging capabilities.

The ConTest flow is depicted in Fig. 9. Given an SUT and a set of test cases (pre-existing or generated by a test generation tool), ConTest first instruments the SUT to allow noise/delay to be injected to relevant program points. The test-cases are ordered using a heuristic, and then run. For each test case, different schedules will be tried. In case that a bug was exposed it is fixed (externally to ConTest) and the system can later be re-tested under ConTest. The ordering is saved, and every execution produces a trace. Both are used to replay a failing test case, to the point where the bug is exposed. In case that no bug was exposed, the ordering is changed by ConTest to cause new interleavings. This cycle is repeated until some concurrency-relevant coverage is reached, or until we run out of time.

7   Case Studies

Within the FITTEST project we have carried out case studies at four different companies, comprising of in total eight studies, in order to evaluate all the tools presented in Sects. 2–6. The section gives an overview of the case studies; for the details of these studies we will refer to their respective reports. The companies (IBM, SOFTEAM, Sulake, and Clavei) indicated different needs for our tools, as shown below:

	IBM	SOFTEAM	Sulake	Clavei
Continuous testing tools	√	√		
Regression testing tool	√			
Combinatoric testing tools	√	√	√	
Rogue user testing tool		√		√
Concurrency testing tool			√	

We did not manage to complete the evaluation of the concurrency tool at Sulake, as the company left the project before we could finish the study.

7.1   Evaluation Framework

To be able to evaluate the FITTEST testing tools in such a way as to assure that the resulting body of evidence can yield the right guidelines for software testing practitioners about which tool fits his or her needs and which does not, the evaluative case studies should:

- involve realistic systems and subjects, and not toy-programs and students as is the case in most current work [52,53],
- be done with thoroughness to ensure that any benefit identified during the evaluation study is clearly derived from the testing technique studied,
- ensure that different studies can be compared.

In order to simplify the design of case studies for comparing software testing techniques while ensuring that the many guidelines and check-list for doing empirical work have been met, we have defined a general methodological framework in FITTEST that can be found in [54]. The framework we have developed has evolved throughout the past years by doing case studies to evaluate testing techniques. The need to have a framework as described in this paper emerged some years ago during the execution of the EU funded project EvoTest (IST-33472, 2007–2009, [55]) and continued emerging during the EU funded project FITTEST (ICT-257574, 2010–2013, [56]). Both these are projects whose objectives are the development of testing tools that somewhere in the project need to be evaluated within industrial environments. Searching in the existing literature to find a framework that could be applied in our situation, did not result in anything that exactly fit our need: a *methodological* framework that is specific enough for the evaluation of software testing techniques and general enough and not make any assumptions about the testing technique that is being evaluated nor about the subjects and the pilot projects. We needed a framework that can be instantiated for any type of treatment, subject and object and simplifies the design of evaluative studies by suggesting relevant questions and measures. Since such a framework did not exist, we defined our own making sure that the guidelines and checklist that can be found in the literature are satisfied. We have successfully used the framework for the various case studies executed during EvoTest and during FITTEST.

7.2 The Case Studies

IBM Research Lab in Haifa. Three case studies are executed at IBM Research Lab in Haifa: (1) automated test cases generation with the FITTEST ITE [57], (2) regression testing [58], and (3) combinatorial testing with the CTE [59]. The studies were done amongst the research team responsible for building the testing environment for future developments of an IT Management Product (IMP) (similar to [60]), a resource management system in a networked environment. At IBM Research Lab, the developers conduct limited amount of testing, the testing itself is conducted by this designated research team. It is working to enable the testing of new versions of the IMP by developing a simulated environment in which the system is executed.

The testing activities, related to the studies, have been done on IMP but in a simulated testing environment. The objective of the team was to identify whether current testing practices could be improved or complemented by using some of the new testing techniques that were introduced by the FITTEST EU project. For this purpose, the IBM Research team has used the FITTEST tools and compared the results with the testing practices currently used during the initial steps of the Systems Verification Test (SVT). Only this level of tests was considered, since the next stage of the SVT testing is conducted elsewhere in IBM and so is beyond the case studies.

Finally, since the IMP is a mature system, and in order to be able to measure fault-finding capability, several faults were injected into it within the simulated environment to mimic potential problems that had can be surfaced in such a system.

Details and results of these studies can be found in: [57–59].

SOFTEAM is a private software vendor and engineering company with about 700 employees located in Paris, France. Three case studies are conducted in this company: (1) automated test cases generation with the FITTEST ITE [61], (2) combinatorial testing with the CTE [62, 63], and (3) rogue user testing [64]. The studies were done within the development team responsible for Modelio Saas, a rather new SOFTEAM product. The team is composed of 1 project manager, 2 software developers and 3 software analysts.

Modelio SaaS is a web application written in PHP that allows for the easy configuration of distributed environments. It runs in virtualized environments on different cloud platforms presenting a high number of configurations and hence presents various challenges to testing [9]. We focus on the Web administration console, which allows administrators to manage projects created with the Modelio modeling tool [10], and to specify allowed users for working on projects. The source code is composed of 50 PHP files with a total of 2141 lines of executable code.

Currently at SOFTEAM, Modelio SaaS test cases are designed manually. The process is based on a series of specified use-cases to support exploratory testing. As indicated before, the objective of test design is to maximize use-case coverage. Each test case describes a sequence of user interactions with the graphical user interface.

Details and results of these studies can be found in: [61–64].

Sulake is a Finnish company that develops social entertainment games and communities whose main product is Habbo Hotel (see footnote 2). The case study executed at Sulake was related to combinatorial testing with the CTE of Habbo is the world's largest virtual community for teenagers. Localized Habbo communities are visited by millions of teenagers every week all around the world [65].

Habbo Hotel can be accessed via the local Habbo sites, and through Facebook, where all 11 of Habbo Hotel's language versions are also available. Through Facebook Connect, Habbo users around the world can easily find their Facebook friends in the virtual world and share their in-world experiences. Some quick Habbo facts (from 2011): 11 language versions; Customers in over 150 countries; Registered users: 218.000.000; Unique visitors: more than 11.000.000 per month; 90 % of the users between the age of 13–18. Combinatorial testing for a system such a Habbo is a challenging task, since there exists a wide variety of operating systems and browsers (and their different versions) used by players. Currently, at Sulake, testing new features is planned using high level feature charters to support exploratory testing and automated regression tests are designed for most critical use cases identified during exploratory testing. Teams make sure that the developed features have automated regression tests. Besides feature coverage, test engineers (and their teams) are provided user information that contains for example % of users using each browser, operating system and flash player version. This information is used to take combinatorial aspects into account and design the tests in such a way that user variables that cover most users' setups are tested. For example, when a test is being designed that needs more than one browser (e.g. a friend request from user A to B), this user information is used to make sure that two different user set-up (one for A and one for B) are configured in such a way that most popular user configurations are tested.

Habbo is built on highly scalable client-server technology. The Action-Script 3 client communicates with a Java server cluster to support tens of thousands of concurrent, interactive users. The server cluster is backed by a MySQL database and intensive caching solutions to guarantee performance under heavy load. The game client is implemented with AS3 and takes care of room rendering, user to user interactions, navigation, purchasing UIs etc. Client performance is challenging as it has to handle up to 50 moving, dancing, talking characters with disco balls, fireworks and user defined game logic running real time in AS3. The game server is a standalone JavaSE with game logic fully implemented in server side. The server handles 10K+ messages/second and Habbo runs as highly distributed system with dedicated role- based clusters, the largest instances having over 100 JVMs. Habbo website and tools are built on Java/Struts2 with AJAX, CSS etc and run on Tomcats.

Details and results of this study can be found in [65].

Clavei is a private software vendor from Alicante (Spain), which specializes in Enterprise Resource Planning (ERP) systems. One of their main products is called *ClaveiCon* and is used in small and medium-sized companies within Spain.

Due to their many clients, it is of fundamental importance to Clavei to thoroughly test their application before releasing a new version. Currently, this is done manually. Due to the complexity and size of the application this is a time-consuming and daunting task. Therefore, Clavei is eager to investigate alternative, more automated approaches to reduce the testing burden for their employees and hence participated in an evaluation of the FITTEST Rogue User Testing tool.

The company, not being part of the FITTEST consortium, expressed explicit interest in the FITTEST Rogue User Tool and requested to carry out a trial period to investigate the applicability of the tool for testing their ERP products; details and results of this study can be found in [66].

8 Conclusion and Future Work

With our continuous testing tools it is possible to log the execution of an application, and from the gathered logs to infer a behavior model of the application, and properties that can be used as test oracles. Combinatoric test sequences can be generated from the model to be used as test cases. Strategies, e.g. a search-based approach, can be applied if these sequences need non-trivial reachability predicates to be solved. The usage of these tools can in principle be scripted so that they work in unattended cycles. However, the challenge is then to evolve the previously obtained models and properties when we advance to the new cycle, rather than to just discard them. This is not just a matter of efficiency. The new cycle may not cover all functionalities covered in the previous cycles; we lose information if we simply discard previous models. On the other hand, it is also possible that some old functionalities have been removed. This calls for some strategy in evolving the models, e.g. based on some assumption on expiration time of the models [10]; this is left as future work.

Our CSTP tool can be used to inject artificial mutations on service responses, and then used to rank test-cases based on their sensitivity to the mutations. This is useful in regression testing, to prioritize test cases when time and budget are limited. In the case study at IBM, the resulting prioritization is as good as a manual prioritization made by an expert [58]. In a separate case study, just using 10 % of the test cases (in total 159) ranked by CSTP we can detect four out of five injected faults [23].

We have improved the combinatoric testing tool CTE XL with new features, e.g. ability to prioritize its test cases generation based on weight assigned to elements of the used classification tree [35], and ability to generate sequences of elementary test cases [36]. The latter is also essential for Internet applications, which are often event-based. An execution of such an application is a sequence of user events, each may have parameters. So, a test case for such an application is also a sequence. The case studies at IBM, SOFTEAM, and Sulake indicated that test cases generated by CTE can find errors that were not discovered by manual test cases [59,63]. However CTE test cases also left some features uncovered [65]. In a way, this is as expected. A domain expert would know how to activate a given set of target features, whereas CTE would do better in systematically exploring patches in the search space. A possible future work is to use available manual test cases as directives when generating combinatoric test cases.

Generating the specified kinds of combinations can however be non-trivial, in particular when there are constraints on which combinations are valid. There are various heuristics to do this, but their performance also depends on the kind of problem we have at hand. Our Hyperheuristic Search-based tool generates combinations by learning the right composition of its lower level heuristics. A study has been carried out, showing that this approach is general, effective, and is able to learn as the problem set changes [46]. This approach is however not yet incorporated in either CTE nor Focus CTD; this is future work.

Our rogue user tool can do robustness testing on Internet applications from their GUIs. The tool is fully automatic; it explores the GUI to try to crash the target application, or to make it violates some pre-specified oracles. In the case studies at Clavei and SOFTTEAM the tool was able to find critical errors that were not found before [64,66].

For concurrency testing, we have improved ConTest with a number of important features: it can now be used to test at the system level, it can generate load, and it can record and replay. It is now thus suitable to test Internet applications, which often form distributed systems (e.g. multiple servers with multiple clients). Using the new record-and-replay functionality we can first record events and messages, and then replay them at desired levels of intensity to generate load that can expose concurrency bugs at a network level.

When an execution fails, it may still be non-trivial to find the root cause of the failure. This is especially true for Internet applications which are often event-based. An execution of such an application can be long, driven by a sequence of top-level events. When the execution fails, simply inspecting the content of the call stack, as we usually do when debugging, may not reveal the root cause, since the stack only explained what the *last* top-level event did. In the FITTEST project we have also investigated this problem. In [14] we use the pattern-based oracles inferred by the continuous testing tools to reduce the log belonging to a failing execution, thus making it easier to be inspected. The reduction tries to filter out events irrelevant to the failure, and preserves the last logged abstract state of the execution, where the failure is observed. The approach works off-line; it is fast, but is inherently inaccurate. We then investigated if combining it with an on-line approach such as delta debugging [67] will give us a better result. Our preliminary investigation shows a promising result [68]. Ultimately, the performance depends on how well the chosen state abstraction used by the logger is related to the failure. Deciding what information to be included in the state abstraction is not trivial, and is left as future work. The above approaches help us in figuring out which top-level events are at least related to the failure. A more refined analysis can be applied, e.g. spectra analysis [69], if we also know e.g. which lines of code are passed by the failing execution. This requires tracing; but when applied on a production system we should also consider the incurred overhead. In [70] we proposed a novel tracing approach with very low overhead, at least for single threaded executions. Extending the approach to multi threads setup is future work.

Acknowledgments. This work has been funded by the European Union FP7 project FITTEST (grant agreement n. 257574). The work presented in this paper is due to the contributions of many researchers, among which Sebastian Bauersfeld, Nelly O. Condori, Urko Rueda, Arthur Baars, Roberto Tiella, Cu Duy Nguyen, Alessandro Marchetto, Alex Elyasov, Etienne Brosse, Alessandra Bagnato, Kiran Lakhotia, Yue Jia, Bilha Mendelson, Daniel Citron and Joachim Wegener.

References

1. Vos, T., Tonella, P., Wegener, J., Harman, M., Prasetya, I.S.W.B., Ur, S.: Testing of future internet applications running in the cloud. In: Tilley, S., Parveen, T. (eds.) Software Testing in the Cloud: Perspectives on an Emerging Discipline, pp. 305–321. IGI Global, Hershey (2013)

2. Prasetya, I.S.W.B., Elyasov, A., Middelkoop, A., Hage, J.: FITTEST log format (version 1.1). Technical report UUCS-2012-014, Utrecht University (2012)
3. Middelkoop, A., Elyasov, A.B., Prasetya, W.: Functional instrumentation of ActionScript programs with Asil. In: Gill, A., Hage, J. (eds.) IFL 2011. LNCS, vol. 7257, pp. 1–16. Springer, Heidelberg (2012)
4. Swierstra, S.D., et al.: UU Attribute Grammar System (1998). https://www.cs.uu.nl/foswiki/HUT/AttributeGrammarSystem
5. Dias Neto, A.C., Subramanyan, R., Vieira, M., Travassos, G.H.: A survey on model-based testing approaches: a systematic review. In: 1st ACM International Workshop on Empirical Assessment of Software Engineering Languages and Technologies, pp. 31–36. ACM, New York (2007)
6. Shafique, M., Labiche, Y.: A systematic review of model based testing tool support. Technical report SCE-10-04, Carleton University, Canada (2010)
7. Marchetto, A., Tonella, P., Ricca, F.: ReAjax: a reverse engineering tool for Ajax web applications. Softw. IET 6(1), 33–49 (2012)
8. Babenko, A., Mariani, L., Pastore, F.: AVA: automated interpretation of dynamically detected anomalies. In: Proceedings of the International Symposium on Software Testing and Analysis (2009)
9. Dallmeier, V., Lindig, C., Wasylkowski, A., Zeller, A.: Mining object behavior with ADABU. In: Proceedings of the International Workshop on Dynamic Systems Analysis (2006)
10. Mariani, L., Marchetto, A., Nguyen, C.D., Tonella, P., Baars, A.I.: Revolution: automatic evolution of mined specifications. In: ISSRE, pp. 241–250 (2012)
11. Nguyen, C.D., Tonella, P.: Automated inference of classifications and dependencies for combinatorial testing. In: Proceedings of the 28th IEEE/ACM International Conference on Automated Software Engineering, ASE (2013)
12. Ernst, M.D., Perkins, J.H., Guo, P.J., McCamant, S., Pacheco, C., Tschantz, M.S., Xiao, C.: The daikon system for dynamic detection of likely invariants. Sci. Comput. Program. 69, 35–45 (2007)
13. Elyasov, A., Prasetya, I.S.W.B., Hage, J.: Guided algebraic specification mining for failure simplification. In: Yenigün, H., Yilmaz, C., Ulrich, A. (eds.) ICTSS 2013. LNCS, vol. 8254, pp. 223–238. Springer, Heidelberg (2013)
14. Elyasov, A., Prasetya, I.S.W.B., Hage, J.: Log-based reduction by rewriting. Technical report UUCS-2012-013, Utrecht University (2012)
15. Prasetya, I.S.W.B., Hage, J., Elyasov, A.: Using sub-cases to improve log-based oracles inference. Technical report UUCS-2012-012, Utrecht University (2012)
16. Anon.: The daikon invariant detector user manual (2010). https://groups.csail.mit.edu/pag/daikon/download/doc/daikon.html
17. Nguyen, C.D., Marchetto, A., Tonella, P.: Combining model-based and combinatorial testing for effective test case generation. In: Proceedings of the 2012 International Symposium on Software Testing and Analysis, pp. 100–110. ACM (2012)
18. Tonella, P.: FITTEST deliverable D4.3: test data generation and UML2 profile (2013)
19. Fraser, G., Arcuri, A.: EvoSuite: automatic test suite generation for object-oriented software. In: Proceedings of the 13th Conference on Foundations of Software Engineering, ESEC/FSE, pp. 416–419. ACM, New York (2011)
20. Rothermel, G., Harrold, M.J.: A safe, efficient regression test selection technique. ACM Trans. Softw. Eng. Methodol. 6(2), 173–210 (1997)
21. Rothermel, G., Untch, R.H., Chu, C., Harrold, M.J.: Prioritizing test cases for regression testing. IEEE Trans. Softw. Eng. 27, 929–948 (2001)

22. W3C: Web service description language (WSDL). Technical report. http://www. w3.org/tr/wsdl20. Accessed Dec 2010

23. Nguyen, D.C., Marchetto, A., Tonella, P.: Change sensitivity based prioritization for audit testing of webservice compositions. In: Proceedings of the 6th International Workshop on Mutation Analysis (co-located with ICST), pp. 357–365 (2011)

24. Ludwig, H., Keller, A., Dan, A., King, R., Franck, R.: A service level agreement language for dynamic electronic services. Electron. Commer. Res. **3**, 43–59 (2003). doi:10.1023/A:1021525310424

25. W3C: XML path language (XPath). Technical report (1999). http://www.w3.org/ tr/xpath/

26. W3C: XML schema. Technical report. http://www.w3.org/xml/schema. Accessed Dec 2010

27. Cohen, M.B., Snyder, J., Rothermel, G.: Testing across configurations: implications for combinatorial testing. SIGSOFT Softw. Eng. Notes **31**, 1–9 (2006)

28. Kuhn, D.R., Wallace, D.R., Gallo, A.M.: Software fault interactions and implications for software testing. IEEE Trans. Softw. Eng. **30**, 418–421 (2004)

29. Grochtmann, M., Grimm, K.: Classification trees for partition testing. Softw. Test. Verif. Reliab. **3**(2), 63–82 (1993)

30. Kruse, P.M., Bauer, J., Wegener, J.: Numerical constraints for combinatorial interaction testing. In: Proceedings of ICST 2012 Workshops (ICSTW 2012), Montreal, Canada (2012)

31. Grochtmann, M., Wegener, J.: Test case design using classification trees and the classification-tree editor CTE. In: Proceedings of the 8th International Software Quality Week, San Francisco, USA (1995)

32. Lehmann, E., Wegener, J.: Test case design by means of the CTE XL. In: Proceedings of the 8th European International Conference on Software Testing, Analysis & Review (EuroSTAR 2000), Kopenhagen, Denmark, Citeseer (2000)

33. Nie, C., Leung, H.: A survey of combinatorial testing. ACM Comput. Surv. **43**, 11:1–11:29 (2011)

34. Kruse, P.M., Luniak, M.: Automated test case generation using classification trees. Softw. Qual. Prof. **13**(1), 4–12 (2010)

35. Kruse, P.M., Schieferdecker, I.: Comparison of approaches to prioritized test generation for combinatorial interaction testing. In: Federated Conference on Computer Science and Information Systems (FedCSIS) 2012, Wroclaw, Poland (2012)

36. Kruse, P.M., Wegener, J.: Test sequence generation from classification trees. In: Proceedings of ICST 2012 Workshops (ICSTW 2012), Montreal, Canada (2012)

37. Kruse, P.M., Lakhotia, K.: Multi objective algorithms for automated generation of combinatorial test cases with the classification tree method. In: Symposium on Search Based Software Engineering (SSBSE 2011) (2011)

38. Ferrer, J., Kruse, P.M., Chicano, J.F., Alba, E.: Evolutionary algorithm for prioritized pairwise test data generation. In: Proceedings of Genetic and Evolutionary Computation Conference (GECCO) 2012, Philadelphia, USA (2012)

39. Prasetya, I.S.W.B., Amorim, J., Vos, T., Baars, A.: Using Haskell to script combinatoric testing of web services. In: 6th Iberian Conference on Information Systems and Technologies (CISTI). IEEE (2011)

40. Cohen, D.M., Dalal, S.R., Fredman, M.L., Patton, G.C.: The AETG system: an approach to testing based on combinatorial design. IEEE Trans. Softw. Eng. **23**(7), 437–444 (1997)

41. Cohen, M.B., Gibbons, P.B., Mugridge, W.B., Colbourn, C.J.: Constructing test suites for interaction testing. In: Proceedings of the 25th International Conference

on Software Engineering, ICSE '03, pp. 38–48. IEEE Computer Society, Washington, DC (2003)

42. Hnich, B., Prestwich, S., Selensky, E., Smith, B.: Constraint models for the covering test problem. Constraints **11**, 199–219 (2006)

43. Lei, Y., Tai, K.: In-parameter-order: a test generation strategy for pairwise testing. In: Proceedings of the 3rd IEEE International Symposium on High-Assurance Systems Engineering, 1998, pp. 254–261 (1998)

44. Garvin, B., Cohen, M., Dwyer, M.: Evaluating improvements to a meta-heuristic search for constrained interaction testing. Emp. Softw. Eng. **16**(1), 61–102 (2011)

45. Calvagna, A., Gargantini, A.: A formal logic approach to constrained combinatorial testing. J. Autom. Reasoning **45**, 331–358 (2010)

46. Jia, Y., Cohen, M.B., Harman, M., Petke, J.: Learning combinatorial interaction testing strategies using hyperheuristic search. Technical report RN/13/17, Department of Computer Sciences, University of College London (2013)

47. Harman, M., Burke, E., Clark, J., Yao, X.: Dynamic adaptive search based software engineering. In: Proceedings of the ACM-IEEE International Symposium on Empirical Software Engineering and Measurement, ESEM '12, pp. 1–8 (2012)

48. Burke, E.K., Gendreau, M., Hyde, M., Kendall, G., Ochoa, G., Ozcan, E., Qu, R.: Hyper-heuristics: a survey of the state of the art. J. Oper. Res. Soc. **64**(12), 1695–1724 (2013)

49. Bauersfeld, S., Vos, T.E.J.: GUITest: a Java library for fully automated GUI robustness testing. In: Proceedings of the 27th IEEE/ACM International Conference on Automated Software Engineering, ASE 2012, pp. 330–333. ACM, New York (2012)

50. Bauersfeld, S., Vos, T.E.: A reinforcement learning approach to automated GUI robustness testing. In: 4th Symposium on Search Based-Software Engineering, p. 7 (2012)

51. Edelstein, O., Farchi, E., Goldin, E., Nir, Y., Ratsaby, G., Ur, S.: Framework for testing multithreaded java programs. Concur. Comput. Pract. Exp. **15**(3–5), 485–499 (2003)

52. Juristo, N., Moreno, A., Vegas, S.: Reviewing 25 years of testing technique experiments. Emp. Softw. Eng. **9**(1–2), 7–44 (2004)

53. Hesari, S., Mashayekhi, H., Ramsin, R.: Towards a general framework for evaluating software development methodologies. In: Proceedings of 34th IEEE COMPSAC, pp. 208–217 (2010)

54. Vos, T.E.J., Marín, B., Escalona, M.J., Marchetto, A.: A methodological framework for evaluating software testing techniques and tools. In: 12th International Conference on Quality Software, Xi'an, China, 27–29 August 2012, pp. 230–239 (2012)

55. Vos, T.E.J.: Evolutionary testing for complex systems. ERCIM News **2009**(78) (2009)

56. Vos, T.E.J.: Continuous evolutionary automated testing for the future internet. ERCIM News **2010**(82), 50–51 (2010)

57. Nguyen, C., Mendelson, B., Citron, D., Shehory, O., Vos, T., Condori-Fernandez, N.: Evaluating the fittest automated testing tools: an industrial case study. In: 2013 ACM/IEEE International Symposium on Empirical Software Engineering and Measurement, pp. 332–339 (2013)

58. Nguyen, C., Tonella, P., Vos, T., Condori, N., Mendelson, B., Citron, D., Shehory, O.: Test prioritization based on change sensitivity: an industrial case study. Technical report UU-CS-2014-012, Utrecht University (2014)

59. Shehory, O., Citron, D., Kruse, P.M., Fernandez, N.C., Vos, T.E.J., Mendelson, B.: Assessing the applicability of a combinatorial testing tool within an industrial environment. In: Proceedings of the 11th Workshop on Experimental Software Engineering (ESELAW 2014), CiBSE (2014)
60. http://pic.dhe.ibm.com/infocenter/director/pubs/index.jsp?topic=%2Fcom.ibm.director.vim.helps.doc%2Ffsd0_vim_main.html
61. Brosse, E., Bagnato, A., Vos, T., Condori-Fernandez, N.: Evaluating the FITTEST automated testing tools in SOFTEAM: an industrial case study. Technical report UU-CS-2014-009, Utrecht University (2014)
62. Kruse, P., Condori-Fernandez, N., Vos, T., Bagnato, A., Brosse, E.: Combinatorial testing tool learnability in an industrial environment. In: 2013 ACM/IEEE International Symposium on Empirical Software Engineering and Measurement, pp. 304–312 (2013)
63. Condori-Fernández, N., Vos, T., Kruse, P., Brosse, E., Bagnato, A.: Analyzing the applicability of a combinatorial testing tool in an industrial environment. Technical report UU-CS-2014-008, Utrecht University (2014)
64. Bauersfeld, S., Condori-Fernandez, N., Vos, T., Brosse, E.: Evaluating rogue user an industrial case study at softeam. Technical report UU-CS-2014-010, Utrecht University (2014)
65. Puoskari, E., Vos, T.E.J., Condori-Fernandez, N., Kruse, P.M.: Evaluating applicability of combinatorial testing in an industrial environment: a case study. In: Proceedings of the JAMAICA, pp. 7–12. ACM (2013)
66. Bauersfeld, S., de Rojas, A., Vos, T.: Evaluating rogue user testing in industry: an experience report. Technical report UU-CS-2014-011, Utrecht University (2014)
67. Zeller, A.: Isolating cause-effect chains from computer programs. In: 10th ACM SIGSOFT symposium on Foundations of Software Engineering (FSE), pp. 1–10 (2002)
68. Elyasov, A., Prasetya, I., Hage, J., Nikas, A.: Reduce first, debug later. In: Proceedings of ICSE 2014 Workshops - 9th International Workshop on Automation of Software Test (AST 2014). ACM-IEEE, Washington, DC (2014)
69. Naish, L., Lee, H.J., Ramamohanarao, K.: A model for spectra-based software diagnosis. ACM Trans. Softw. Eng. Methodol **20**(3), 11:1–11:32 (2011)
70. Prasetya, I.S.W.B., Sturala, A., Middelkoop, A., Hage, J., Elyasov, A.: Compact traceable logging. In: 5th International Conference on Advances in System Testing and Validation (VALID) (2013)
71. Tonella, P., Marchetto, A., Nguyen, C.D., Jia, Y., Lakhotia, K., Harman, M.: Finding the optimal balance between over and under approximation of models inferred from execution logs. In: Proceedings of the Fifth IEEE International Conference on Software Testing, Verification and Validation (ICST), pp. 21–30 (2012)

Assessing the Impact of Firewalls and Database Proxies on SQL Injection Testing

Dennis Appelt[✉], Nadia Alshahwan, and Lionel Briand

Interdisciplinary Centre for Security, Reliability and Trust,
University of Luxembourg, Luxembourg, Luxembourg
{dennis.appelt,nadia.alshahwan,lionel.briand}@uni.lu

Abstract. This paper examines the effects and potential benefits of utilising Web Application Firewalls (WAFs) and database proxies in SQL injection testing of web applications and services. We propose testing the WAF itself to refine and evaluate its security rules and prioritise fixing vulnerabilities that are not protected by the WAF. We also propose using database proxies as oracles for black-box security testing instead of relying only on the output of the application under test. The paper also presents a case study of our proposed approaches on two sets of web services. The results indicate that testing through WAFs can be used to prioritise vulnerabilities and that an oracle that uses a database proxy finds more vulnerabilities with fewer tries than an oracle that relies only on the output of the application.

Keywords: SQL injections · Blackbox testing · Web services

1 Introduction

In recent years, the world wide web evolved from a static source of information to an important application platform. Banking, shopping, education, social networking and even government processes became available through the web. The rise of cloud-backed applications and web-centric operating systems like Windows 8 or Chrome OS further accelerated this shift.

The popularity of web applications can be attributed to their continuous availability, accessibility and flexibility. However, this also caused the web to become a target for malicious attackers. Recent studies found that the number of reported web vulnerabilities is growing sharply [11]. Web applications experience, on average, 27 attacks per hour [4].

Web technologies, such as HTML5, are constantly developing to enable the production of richer web applications and enhance user experience. However, with new functionality comes a higher risk of introducing vulnerabilities [15,22]. Developers might be unaware of the newest security concepts and unintentionally introduce risks to their applications. Attackers, on the other hand, might misuse new features of web technologies to compromise previously secure applications. These risks raise the need for systematic and well-defined security testing

T.E.J. Vos, K. Lakhotia, and S. Bauersfeld (Eds.): FITTEST 2013, LNCS 8432, pp. 32–47, 2014.
DOI: 10.1007/978-3-319-07785-7_2, © Springer International Publishing Switzerland 2014

approaches that can cope with this constant evolution in security risks. Moreover, with the high pressure of deadlines and limited time and resources allocated to testing, these approaches need to be automated as well as accurate and effective at detecting vulnerabilities.

In addition to testing, practitioners might use several run-time protection mechanisms to protect their applications against attacks, such as Web Application Firewalls (WAFs) and database proxies. WAFs monitor input values received by the application for attack strings while database proxies monitor the communication between the application and the database for suspicious SQL statements. We believe that these two technologies can be utilised in the security testing process and can also affect the results of evaluating different techniques.

In this paper we assess the impact of using WAFs and database proxies on testing for SQL injection vulnerabilities, which are one of the most widely spread types of vulnerabilities [5,24]. We propose that WAFs can be used to prioritise vulnerabilities by focusing developers effort on vulnerabilities that are not protected by the WAF first. We also investigate the effectiveness and efficiency of using database proxies as oracles for SQL injection testing instead of just relying on the output of the application. We expect that using database proxies would enhance the detection rates of vulnerabilities.

The results of our case study on two service-oriented web applications with a total of 33 operations and 108 input parameters indicates that using database proxies as an oracle does indeed improve detection rates. The results also show that detecting vulnerabilities while testing through a WAF is more challenging and that many vulnerabilities are protected by the WAF. This indicates that testing through the WAF can be used to prioritise fixing vulnerabilities in practice.

The rest of this paper is organised as follows: Sect. 2 provides a background on SQL injection testing and presents the definitions of the terms that are used in this paper. Section 3 discusses WAFs and database proxies, whilst Sect. 4 reviews related work. Section 5 presents the case study together with a discussion of results and threats to validity. Finally, Sect. 6 concludes and explores future work.

2   SQL Injection Testing

Existing injection testing approaches can be classified into two main categories: White-box and black-box approaches. These approaches try to detect vulnerabilities caused by poorly validated inputs that an attacker might exploit to cause the application to behave unexpectedly or expose sensitive data. For example, the attacker can construct harmful strings that flow into SQL statements and change their intended behaviour.

White-box approaches use static and dynamic analysis of the source code to detect vulnerabilities. Some White-box approaches track the execution of the program to identify un-validated inputs that flow into SQL statements or output commands [19]. Other approaches use symbolic execution to identify the constraints that need to be satisfied to lead to an SQL injection attack [12]. Shar and Tan [23] used data mining of the source code to predict vulnerabilities.

White-Box approaches require access to the source code of the application, which might not always be possible. Many companies outsource development of their systems or acquire third party components. Although these companies do not have access to the source code, they still need to ensure that their software is secure.

Black-box techniques typically explore a web application to find input fields that are then used to submit malicious inputs to the application. The output is analysed to determine if the attack was successful. Malicious inputs are formed, for example, using fuzzing techniques that generate new inputs from existing patterns of known vulnerabilities [16]. The detection rates of black-box techniques depend significantly on the ability to craft effective inputs.

SQL injection vulnerabilities are one of the most critical and widely spread types of vulnerabilities [5,24]. An attacker targeting this type of vulnerabilities attempts to manipulate the values of input parameters of an application to inject fragments of SQL commands that evade security mechanisms and flow into an SQL statement. The goal is to alter the SQL statement and change its behaviour in a way that could benefit the attacker. For example, the additional SQL code might result in an SQL query returning more data than what was intended by the developer. Such attacks are usually possible because some developers insert the values provided by the user into SQL statements using string concatenation. If these input values are not validated and checked properly for SQL attack patterns, the SQL code they contain will be part of the SQL statement making it possible to change the effect of the statement.

2.1 Definitions

In this section, we precisely define the terms related to SQL injection testing that will be used throughout this paper. Understanding the meaning of terms such as vulnerability, detectable and exploitable might seem intuitive. However, their precise definition might influence the interpretation of results and evaluation of testing techniques. To the best of our knowledge, these terms have not been defined formally in previous research on SQL injection testing.

In most cases, when input values are used in SQL statements, their values are used as data and not as part of the SQL code to be executed. For example, the following SQL statement is a simplified version of a statement found in one of the applications we use in our case study:

```
$sql="Select * From hotelList where country ='".$country."'";
```

The value of the input parameter $country is used to limit the rows returned by the SQL query to hotels located in the country provided by the user. If this input is not properly validated and checked for malicious values, a user can provide an input such as:

```
' ; drop table hotelList;--
```

The result of concatenating this input with the previous SQL statement would be:

```
$sql = "Select * From hotelList where country =" ;
            drop table hotelList;--';
```

When the database server executes this SQL code, the `Select` statement would return no values while the `drop table` statement would delete the table hotelList (if permission to drop tables is not configured correctly on the database level to prevent such actions). The rest of the command will not be executed because it is commented (`--` symbol). The input in this case was interpreted as SQL code rather than data, allowing the user to alter the database causing loss of information and unavailability of the system because the table was deleted. We can define an SQL vulnerability as follows:

Definition 1. *An SQL vulnerability in a system under test is an input parameter where part or all of its value is used in an SQL statement and interpreted as SQL code instead of treated as data in at least one execution of the system.*

Whether all or part of the input parameter value is interpreted as SQL depends on the attack string used and the logic of the application. For example, in the previous SQL statement if the attack string was `Luxembourg'; drop table hotelList;--` then part of the input value (`Luxembourg`) is treated as data while the rest (`drop table hotelList;--`) is interpreted as SQL.

The goal of an SQL injection testing approach is to detect vulnerabilities. Whether a vulnerability is detected or not also depends on the oracle used. Therefore, we can define a detectable vulnerability as follows:

Definition 2. *A detectable SQL vulnerability with regards to an oracle is a vulnerability that can be detected by this oracle.*

In some cases, a vulnerability exists in the system but an attacker might not be able to exploit it. For example, a numeric input might not be validated properly to ensure that only numeric data can be assigned to it. However, a firewall might be configured correctly to block any attack strings submitted to that same input. Therefore, although the attacker can submit string values to this numeric input parameter, which is unintended behaviour, the attacker would not be able to use this vulnerability to gain any benefit. We can define an exploitable SQL vulnerability as follows:

Definition 3. *An exploitable SQL vulnerability is a vulnerability that can be used to cause an information leak, an unauthorised change in the state of the database or system or causes the system to be unavailable.*

Information leakage, changes to the state or system unavailability might not be the only negative effects an attacker can inflict on the system. However, this definition can be extended when needed to include other types of harmful effects. In some cases, deciding if a vulnerability is exploitable can not be done

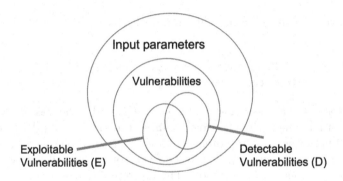

Fig. 1. The different classifications of input parameters to illustrate the relationship between the different classifications.

automatically and requires manual inspection by engineers who have the domain knowledge to decide if a vulnerability is exploitable. For example, a vulnerability in the system might be exploited to leak information but the information that is leaked is not sensitive or can be obtained by any user through alternative methods. However, an automated approach might be able to estimate the probability of a vulnerability being exploitable based on some heuristics. Vulnerabilities can then be ranked based on this probability to reduce the time required for manual inspection or focus efforts on vulnerabilities that might pose a higher threat.

Figure 1 illustrates the relationship between the different classifications of input parameters. A subset of all input parameters might be vulnerable, while a subset of those vulnerabilities is exploitable. Detectable vulnerabilities could either be exploitable or not exploitable. The intersection of detectable vulnerabilities and exploitable vulnerabilities (E ∩ D) is the set of critical security faults that the testing process found. The set of exploitable vulnerabilities that are not detectable (E−D) represents the false negatives of the testing process.

3   Security Mechanisms

Several types of security mechanisms are used at run-time to protect against SQL injection attacks. The two main security mechanisms used in practice are firewalls and database proxies. In the next two sections we examine each type in more detail and discuss their effect and potential utilisation in SQL security testing.

3.1   Web Application Firewalls

A Web Application Firewall (WAF) examines every request submitted by the user to the application to decide if the request should be accepted (when it is a legal request) or rejected (if the request is malicious). The WAF makes this decision by examining each input value in the request and checking if the value matches an attack pattern typically using a set of rules (regular expressions).

The performance of the WAF and the protection it provides depends on this set of rules. Since these rules are created and maintained manually by the application owner, they might be error-prone and security holes might be introduced by mistake. On the other hand, attackers are continually searching for ways to evade firewalls by using mechanisms such as obfuscation where equivalent encodings of attack patterns are used that might not be recognized by the WAF. WAFs are commonly used in the industry, for example, using a WAF is necessary to be compliant with the Payment Card Industry Data Security Standard [20] for systems that use/process credit cards.

Naturally, using a WAF affects the security assessment of an application; some input parameters might be vulnerable if the application is accessed directly but not vulnerable when a WAF is used. For example, an input parameter that flows to an SQL statement might not be validated for SQL injection attack patterns but the WAF is configured to detect and reject such attack patterns. In some cases in practice, all validation and filtering might be delegated to the WAF. Testing applications with such a set-up using approaches that only take into account the application itself and not the WAF might result in determining that all inputs that are used in SQL statements are vulnerable. Ideally all these vulnerabilities should be addressed to provide two layers of protection in case an attacker is able to bypass the WAF. However, with limited time and resources dedicated to testing, which is often the case in the industry, test engineers might want to focus on fixing vulnerabilities that can still be exploited even when using a WAF. Therefore, testing an application for SQL injection vulnerabilities through a WAF can be used to identify and prioritise vulnerabilities that can be detected through the WAF.

Testing through a WAF can also have other useful applications, such as testing the WAF itself. This can be useful, for example, if a choice needs to be made by the application owner between different alternative WAFs. The application can be tested using each WAF and the firewall that provides the most protection can be chosen. Finally, testing the WAF could help in evaluating and refining its rule set. When a vulnerability is found that can be detected while using a WAF, the developers, after fixing the application code to eliminate the vulnerability, can define new rules or adjust existing rules to protect the application against similar types of vulnerabilities. This might be useful to protect the application against similar types of vulnerabilities that might be introduced in subsequent versions of the system.

3.2 Database Proxies

Database proxies (e.g., GreenSQL [13], Snort [21], Apache-scalp [2]) reside between the application and the database and monitor each SQL statement issued from the application to the database for malicious commands. These proxies have an advantage over WAFs in that they have access to the SQL statement after it is formulated and, therefore, have more information to decide if an SQL command is an attack. Database proxies can usually be configured to either a prevention mode where malicious attacks are blocked by the proxy or a monitoring mode where suspicious requests are allowed to execute but logged for further examination by an administrator.

Typically, database proxies use either a risk-based or learning-based approach to decide if an SQL statement is malicious. The risk-based approach assigns a risk score to each intercepted SQL statement which reflects the probability of the statement being malicious. To calculate the risk score, each statement is assessed for SQL fragments frequently used in SQL injection attacks, e.g. the comment sign or a tautology. In the learning based approach, the security engineer first sets the proxy to a learning mode and issues a number of legal requests that represent the application's behaviour. The proxy, thereby, learns the different forms of SQL commands that the application can execute. When the proxy is set to the monitoring or prevention mode, any request that does not comply with these learnt forms is flagged as malicious. The effectiveness of the proxy is dependent on this learning phase: If the requests issued in this phase do not represent all legal behaviour of the application, legal requests might be flagged as suspicious when the proxy is used in practice (high false positive rate).

Existing black-box SQL injection testing approaches commonly use an oracle that relies on the output of the application to decide if a vulnerability was detected [1,6,17]. In this paper we propose using a database proxy as an oracle. Since proxies have access to the SQL statement after all input values have been inserted in the statement and all processing is done, we expect that using the proxy as an oracle would enhance detection rates.

4   Related Work

In this section we briefly review existing techniques for black-box SQL injection testing and also review the results of empirical studies that compare different black-box testing techniques.

Huang et al. [17] proposed a black-box SQL injection approach that learns the application's behaviour and then compares this to the behaviour of the application when SQL injection attacks are submitted. Antunes and Vieira [1] use a similar oracle but focus on SQL and server errors rather than the whole output. For example, if the legal test case led to an SQL or server error but the attack was successful, the approach infers that a vulnerability was found since the attack was able to circumvent the checks that caused the original error. Ciampa et al. [6] analyse the output, including error messages, of both legal and malicious test cases to learn more about the type and structure of the back-end database. This information is then used to craft attack inputs that are more likely to be successful at revealing vulnerabilities. These approaches use an oracle that relies on observing and analysing the output, while we propose using a database proxy as an oracle to enhance detection rates.

Several empirical studies evaluated and compared commercial, open-source and research black-box SQL injection testing tools [3,9,25]. These studies found that black-box testing tools have low detection rates and high false positive rates for SQL injections. This result highlights the need to improve both test generation approaches and oracles for SQL injection testing. In this paper, we focus on improving the oracle by using database proxies rather than relying on the output of the application.

Elia et al. [10] evaluated several intrusion detection tools, including the database proxy GreenSQL that we use in this paper. The study injects security faults into the applications under study and then automatically attacks the application to evaluate the effectiveness of the intrusion detection tools studied. These papers focused on testing and comparing security mechanisms, such as WAFs and database proxies, while we propose utilising these tools in the security testing process.

5   Case Study

We designed the case study to answer the following research questions:

RQ1: What is the impact of using an oracle that observes communications to the database on SQL injection vulnerability detection?

We expect that an oracle that observes the database to determine that a vulnerability was detected might improve the detection rates of an SQL injection testing approach compared to an oracle that only relies on the output. However, using such an oracle might result in a high number of false positives or have other implications on the results. To answer this question, we conduct an experiment where we perform SQL injection testing using a state-of-the-art tool that relies only on the output and a prototype tool that we developed that uses a state-of-the-art database proxy as an oracle. We compare the number of vulnerabilities detected and the number of test cases that needed to be generated before the vulnerability was detected. We also examine the requests that detected vulnerabilities for both approaches to investigate whether they led to the formulation of executable malicious SQL statements and, therefore, led to detecting exploitable vulnerabilities.

RQ2: How does testing the web services directly and testing them through a WAF impact the effectiveness of SQL injection testing?

Generating test cases that are able to detect vulnerabilities in web services through a WAF is naturally expected to be more challenging than testing the application directly, since the WAF provides an additional layer of protection. However, vulnerabilities that can be detected while testing through the WAF pose a more pressing threat since they are completely not protected. To answer this question, we test the application using the two testing approaches (the state-of-the-art tool and our prototype tool) through a state-of-the-art WAF and compare the results to those obtained without using the WAF. A reduction in the number of vulnerabilities found might indicate that testing through the WAF can be used to prioritise fixing vulnerabilities that are not protected by the WAF. Such reduction might also indicate that we need more advanced test generation techniques for security testing that can penetrate the more sophisticated protection techniques of WAFs and identify harder to detect vulnerabilities.

Table 1. Details about the two applications we used in the case study

Application	#Operations	#Parameters	LoC
Hotel reservation service	7	21	1,566
SugarCRM	26	87	352,026
Total	33	108	353,592

5.1 Case Study Subjects

We selected service-based web applications rather than traditional web applications to eliminate the effects of crawling the web application on results. Web services have well-defined and documented APIs that can be used to call the different operations in the application. On the other hand, web applications require a crawling mechanism to be built into the testing technique to explore the application and find input fields that might be vulnerable. The crawling mechanism might impact the effectiveness of the overall testing approach as noted by previous studies [3,9,18].

We chose two open-source service-based applications as subjects for the case study. Table 1 provides information about the number of operations, input parameters and lines of code for the chosen applications. The Hotel Reservation Service was created by researchers[1] to study service-oriented architectures and was used in previous studies [7]. SugarCRM, is a popular customer relationship management system (189+K downloads in 2013[2]). Both applications are implemented using PHP, use a MySQL database and provide a SOAP-based Web Service API.

5.2 Prototype Tool

We developed a prototype tool in Java that uses a set of standard attacks as test cases and a state-of-the-art database proxy as an oracle to help answer our research questions. Specifically, the tool is expected to help verify that an oracle which observes database communications to detect SQL injection vulnerabilities could improve the detection rate of an SQL testing approach. The architecture of the tool is depicted in Fig. 2. The testing process can be divided into three subprocesses: test case generation, delivery mechanism and vulnerability detection.

The *test case generation* process takes a valid test case as input (a test case where input data conforms to the specification of the operation under test). This valid test case is transformed into a malicious test case by replacing one input parameter value at a time with an SQL injection attack chosen from a list of standard attacks. We provided the tool with a list of 137 standard attacks that was compiled by Antunes and Vieira [1] and represents common SQL injection attacks. A parameter is replaced with an SQL attack from the list until a vulnerability is detected or all attacks are used. This process is repeated for each input

[1] http://uwf.edu/nwilde/soaResources/
[2] http://sourceforge.net

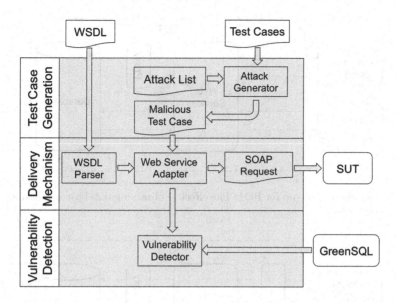

Fig. 2. Architecture of the prototype testing tool.

parameter of the operation under test. The *delivery mechanism* process encapsulates all implementation details which are necessary to deliver the malicious test case to the SOAP-based Web Service and obtain a response. The *vulnerability detection* process uses the state-of-the-art database proxy *GreenSQL* as an oracle to detect vulnerabilities.

GreenSQL is an SQL injection attack detection and prevention tool that supports both the learning-based approach and the risk-based approach discussed in Sect. 3.2. In our case study, we used the learning-based approach to detect malicious SQL statements. We chose GreenSQL based on the results of a previous study that compared GreenSQL to five similar tools and found it to be the most effective in detecting SQL injection attacks [10].

5.3   Case Study Set-up

To perform the case study, we conducted two sets of experiments. In the first set of experiments (Fig. 3), we applied our prototype tool and a state-of-the-art black-box security testing tool that relies only on the output of the application to the two case study subjects. We selected *SqlMap* [8] as a representative for traditional black-box testing tools that rely only on the output. We chose SqlMap because it is an open source free tool that provides support for testing web services as well as web applications. SqlMap is also one of four tools listed on the Open Web Application Security Project (OWASP) website [24] for automated SQL injection testing. The tool was also used in previous studies [6,14].

In the second set of experiments (Fig. 4), we applied the same two tools to our case study subjects but tested the applications through a WAF to answer RQ2. We selected *ModSecurity* for our experiments. ModSecurity is a WAF that

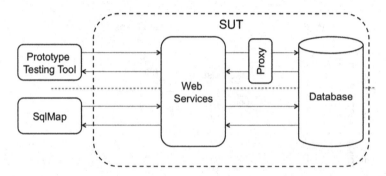

Fig. 3. Experimental set-up for RQ1: The effect of observing database communications on detection rates.

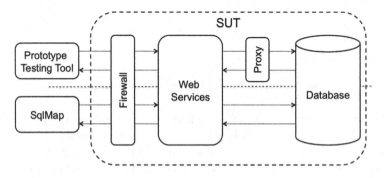

Fig. 4. Experimental set-up for RQ2: The influence of testing through a Web Application Firewall.

protects web servers (Apache, IIS, Nginx) from common threats including SQL injections. Since ModSecurity requires a rule set to identify and reject attacks as discussed in Sect. 3.1, in our case study we used the OWASP [24] core rule set (version 2.2.7).

Our prototype tool is deterministic, therefore we ran the tool once on each application and for each set-up. SqlMap, on the other hand, is not deterministic, therefore we ran the tool 30 times for each application and each set-up. We used the default configuration for SqlMap, except for a minor modification that omits test cases that cause the database to pause the execution of a query, for example by calling the `sleep()` operation, to avoid long execution times.

5.4   Results

This section discusses the results of running the experiments that we described in the previous section on each of the two case study applications. For each experiment, we counted the number of vulnerabilities found by each tool and the number of tries (requests) that the tool needed to generate and execute before finding each vulnerability. As we mentioned before, SqlMap is non-deterministic,

Table 2. Collected data for the described experiments.

Application	Firewall	Prototype		SqlMap	
		#Vulner.	avg. # tries	#Vulner.	avg. # tries
Hotel reservation	Without	6	6.3	6	1,306.55
Service	With	6	28	0	–
SugarCRM	Without	6	2	3.87	566.77
	With	3	34	0	–

therefore, we repeated any experiments that involve it 30 times and calculated the average number of vulnerabilities and tries.

Table 2 summarises all the results obtained from our experiments. Both the prototype tool and SqlMap were run on the two web service applications once while using a WAF and once without. The results show that the prototype tool, which uses a proxy as an oracle, detects more vulnerabilities than SqlMap, which relies only on the output of the application, for both applications and using both set-ups (with and without WAF). The only exception is the Hotel Reservation Service without a firewall where both tools find the same number (6) of vulnerabilities. Manual inspection showed that none of the vulnerabilities reported by either tool is a false positive. We also observe that the number of tries or test cases that the tool needs to execute before detecting the vulnerability (if a vulnerability is found) is significantly higher for SqlMap compared to the prototype tool (1,306.55 vs 6.3 and 566.77 vs 2). These results indicate that using a database proxy as an oracle for SQL injection testing could improve detection rates and could also enhance the efficiency of the testing process by detecting vulnerabilities faster.

The difference in the number of detected vulnerabilities when testing with and without a WAF can help us answer RQ2. As we expected, testing through a WAF is more challenging and both testing tools find fewer vulnerabilities in both applications. The only exception is the result of the prototype tool for the Hotel Reservation Service, where the tool found the same number of vulnerabilities with and without a firewall. SqlMap was unable to detect any vulnerabilities for both applications when using a firewall. We also noticed that when vulnerabilities are found, the number of tries needed to find the vulnerabilities also significantly increased (34 vs 2 and 28 vs 6.3). The prototype tool found three vulnerabilities when testing through the WAF for the SugarCRM application. Therefore, these three vulnerabilities are unprotected by the WAF and any debugging or fault repairing effort should be first focused on these three vulnerabilities since the risk of them being exploited is higher. Another conclusion we might draw from these results is that we need more sophisticated test generation techniques and oracles for SQL injection testing. SqlMap, a state-of-the-art-tool, was unable to find any vulnerabilities in both applications when using a WAF, while our prototype tool detected six in one application and three out of six in the other. A more sophisticated test generation technique might be able to detect vulnerabilities not found by either tool. Moreover, as hackers are continuously searching for new ways and attack patterns to penetrate WAFs and find security holes in applications, SQL injection testing should attempt to emulate these attackers and identify vulnerabilities before the attackers do.

As we noticed in the results that the prototype tool finds only three out of the six vulnerabilities in the SugarCRM application, we investigated the reasons and the difference, if any, between the detected and undetected vulnerabilities when using the WAF. Surprisingly, we found that the WAF blocks even the valid request when testing the operations that have the three undetected vulnerabilities. The reason that the valid requests are blocked for these operations is that some of their parameters are formatted as a series of numbers and letters separated by dashes. The rule set we used for ModSecurity (our WAF) includes a rule that blocks any request that contains more than five spacial characters (e.g., hash signs, quotes, dashes), which these input parameters trigger causing the request to be blocked. We expect such cases to not happen in practice in real systems: Security engineers would customise the configuration and rule set of the WAF to ensure that the normal operations and functionality of the application are not affected. This highlights the need for using real industrial case studies when evaluating tools and techniques to obtain more realistic results that reflect what happens in real systems and contexts. Such studies are unfortunately very rare in the research literature.

We also examined the test cases that successfully detected vulnerabilities when using our prototype tool. We found that these test cases changed the structure of the SQL statements they affected causing GreenSQL to flag them as SQL injection attacks. However, we also found that the resulting SQL statements were not executable. For example, one of the attack strings used that detected a vulnerability was ' UNION SELECT. The vulnerable SQL statement was:

```
$sql="Select * From hotelList where country ='".$country.'"';
```

The SQL statement after injecting the variable $country with the attack string ' UNION SELECT would be:

```
Select * From hotelList where country =' ' UNION SELECT'
```

GreenSQL will detect this statement as an SQL injection attack since the structure of this statement differs from the previously learnt statements. However, the statement itself is not executable and would cause the database server to raise a syntax error when attempting to execute the statement. If the resulting SQL statement was syntactically correct and executable, we might be able to have more confidence in that the detected vulnerability is exploitable. If one of the test cases that detected the vulnerability was used by an attacker, he or she would not be able to gain any benefit from the attack. This suggests that we need to enhance the oracle to get more useful results that can help identify not just detectable vulnerabilities but also exploitable vulnerabilities and produce test cases that result in executable SQL statements that change the behaviour of the application. This can be done, for example, by improving the oracle by combining the database proxy with an additional oracle that checks the syntactical correctness of the resulting SQL statement.

5.5   Threats to Validity

This section discusses the threats to validity of our results in this study using the standard classification of threats [26]:

Internal Threats: The internal threats to validity in this study are related to generation of test cases and the stopping criterion of each approach when studying the effect of the test oracle. Both approaches start from a valid test case when testing each web service operation. We used the same initial test cases for both the prototype tool and SqlMap to avoid experimenter bias.

External Threats: The external threats are related to the choice of case study subjects, the SQL injection testing approaches and the ability to generalise results. Although we only used two systems in the case study, one of the two systems is used by real users as the number of downloads indicates. More experiments with different types of systems might be needed before being able to generalise results. Although we only used two approaches to generate test cases, these two approaches are representative of the state of the art in black-box testing, as the review of related work indicates.

Construct Threats: We used the number of detected vulnerabilities to measure effectiveness and used the number of test cases generated before a vulnerability is detected to measure efficiency. Detecting vulnerabilities is the goal of any SQL injection testing approach, therefore, the number of vulnerabilities seems like the most natural choice to measure effectiveness. The number of requests (or test cases) issued before detecting a vulnerability is a more reliable method of measuring efficiency since execution time might be effected by the environment and/or other processes performed by the CPU while running the experiments.

6   Conclusion

SQL injections are a significant and increasing threat to web applications. It is therefore highly important to test such applications in an effective manner to detect SQL injection vulnerabilities. In many situations, for example when the source code or adequate code analysis technologies are not available, one must resort to black-box testing. This paper examined the impact of Web Application Firewalls (WAFs) and database proxies on black-box SQL injection testing. We proposed using WAFs to prioritise fixing SQL injection vulnerabilities by testing the application with and without using a WAF and then prioritising fixing vulnerabilities that are not protected by the WAF. We also proposed using database proxies, which monitor the communications between the application and the database and flag any suspicious SQL statements, as an oracle for SQL injection testing.

We conducted a case study on two service oriented web applications where we compared the effectiveness and efficiency of two SQL injection tools: SqlMap, which is a state-of-the-art black-box testing tool that uses the output of the application as an oracle and a prototype tool we developed that uses a database proxy (GreenSQL) as an oracle. The results confirmed that using a database proxy increases the detection rates of SQL injection testing and also results in finding vulnerabilities with significantly lower numbers of test cases. A more detailed investigation of the test cases produced revealed that using database proxies helps in detecting more vulnerabilities but a more sophisticated oracle is needed to be able to reason about the vulnerabilities' exploitability, i.e., if an attacker would be able to gain any benefit from the vulnerability.

We also compared the results of the two testing tools when testing through a WAF (ModSecurity) and when testing the applications directly. The results showed that testing through the WAF is more challenging, causing our prototype tool to only detect 50 % of vulnerabilities for one application, while SqlMap detected vulnerabilities for neither application. These results have two implications: Testing through WAFs can be used to prioritise fixing vulnerabilities that are not protected by the WAF. On the other hand, the inability of SqlMap to detect any vulnerabilities when testing through the WAF, although some of those vulnerabilities were detectable by our prototype tool, suggests that we need to improve further both the test generation and oracles of black-box SQL injection testing.

Acknowledgment. This work is supported by the National Research Fund, Luxembourg (FNR/P10/03 and FNR 4800382).

References

1. Antunes, N., Vieira, M.: Detecting SQL injection vulnerabilities in web services. In: Proceedings of the 4th Latin-American Symposium on Dependable Computing (LADC '09), pp. 17–24 (2009)
2. Apache-scalp: Apache log analyzer for security (2008). https://code.google.com/p/apache-scalp
3. Bau, J., Bursztein, E., Gupta, D., Mitchell, J.: State of the art: automated black-box web application vulnerability testing. In: Proceedings of the 2010 IEEE Symposium on Security and Privacy (SP '10), pp. 332–345 (2010)
4. Beery, T., Niv, N.: Web application attack report (2011)
5. Christey, S., Martin, R.A.: Vulnerability type distributions in CVE (2007). http://cwe.mitre.org
6. Ciampa, A., Visaggio, C.A., Di Penta, M.: A heuristic-based approach for detecting SQL-injection vulnerabilities in web applications. In: Proceedings of the ICSE Workshop on Software Engineering for Secure Systems (SESS '10), pp. 43–49 (2010)
7. Coffey, J., White, L., Wilde, N., Simmons, S.: Locating software features in a SOA composite application. In: Proceedings of the 8th IEEE European Conference on Web Services (ECOWS '10), pp. 99–106 (2010)
8. Damele, B., Guimaraes, A., Stampar, M.: Sqlmap (2013). http://sqlmap.org/
9. Doupé, A., Cova, M., Vigna, G.: Why Johnny can't pentest: an analysis of black-box web vulnerability scanners. In: Kreibich, C., Jahnke, M. (eds.) DIMVA 2010. LNCS, vol. 6201, pp. 111–131. Springer, Heidelberg (2010)

10. Elia, I.A., Fonseca, J., Vieira, M.: Comparing SQL injection detection tools using attack injection: an experimental study. In: Proceedings of the IEEE 21st International Symposium on Software Reliability Engineering (ISSRE '10), pp. 289–298 (2010)
11. Fossi, M., Johnson, E.: Symantec global internet security threat report, vol. xiv (2009)
12. Fu, X., Qian, K.: SAFELI: SQL injection scanner using symbolic execution. In: Proceedings of the workshop on Testing, Analysis, and Verification of Web Services and Applications (TAV-WEB '08), pp. 34–39 (2008)
13. GreenSQL LTD: Greensql (2013). http://www.greensql.com
14. Halfond, W.G., Anand, S., Orso, A.: Precise interface identification to improve testing and analysis of web applications. In: Proceedings of the 18th International Symposium on Software Testing and Analysis (ISSTA '09), pp. 285–296 (2009)
15. Hanna, S., Shin, R., Akhawe, D., Boehm, A., Saxena, P., Song, D.: The emperors new apis: on the (in) secure usage of new client-side primitives. In: Proceedings of the Web, vol. 2 (2010)
16. Holler, C., Herzig, K., Zeller, A.: Fuzzing with code fragments. In: Proceedings of the 21st Usenix Security Symposium (2012)
17. Huang, Y.-W., Huang, S.-K., Lin, T.-P., Tsai, C.-H.: Web application security assessment by fault injection and behavior monitoring. In: Proceedings of the 12th International Conference on World Wide Web (WWW '03), pp. 148–159 (2003)
18. Khoury, N., Zavarsky, P., Lindskog, D., Ruhl, R.: Testing and assessing web vulnerability scanners for persistent SQL injection attacks. In: Proceedings of the 1st International Workshop on Security and Privacy Preserving in e-Societies (SeceS '11), pp. 12–18 (2011)
19. Kieyzun, A., Guo, P.J., Jayaraman, K., Ernst, M.D.: Automatic creation of SQL injection and cross-site scripting attacks. In: Proceedings of the 31st International Conference on Software Engineering (ICSE '09), pp. 199–209 (2009)
20. PCI Security Standards Council: Pci data security standard (PCI DSS) (2013). https://www.pcisecuritystandards.org
21. Roesch, M.: Snort - lightweight intrusion detection for networks. In: Proceedings of the 13th USENIX Conference on System Administration, pp. 229–238 (1999)
22. Ryck, P.D., Desmet, L., Philippaerts, P., Piessens, F.: A security analysis of next generation web standards (2011)
23. Shar, L.K., Tan, H.B.K.: Mining input sanitization patterns for predicting SQL injection and cross site scripting vulnerabilities. In: Proceedings of the 34th International Conference on Software Engineering (ICSE NIER '12), pp. 1293–1296 (2012)
24. The Open Web Application Security Project (OWASP): Testing for SQL injection (owasp-dv-005) (2013). http://www.owasp.org
25. Vieira, M., Antunes, N., Madeira, H.: Using web security scanners to detect vulnerabilities in web services. In: Proceedings of the IEEE/IFIP International Conference on Dependable Systems & Networks (DSN'09), pp. 566–571 (2009)
26. Wohlin, C., Runeson, P., Host, M., Ohlsson, M., Regnell, B., Wesslen, A.: The Experimentation in Software Engineering - An Introduction. Kluwer, Dordrecht (2000)

Logging to Facilitate Combinatorial System Testing

Peter M. Kruse[1]([✉]), I.S. Wishnu B. Prasetya[2], Jurriaan Hage[2],
and Alexander Elyasov[2]

[1] Berner and Mattner Systemtechnik GmbH, Berlin, Germany
peter.kruse@berner-mattner.com
[2] Department of Information and Computing Sciences, Utrecht University,
Utrecht, The Netherlands
{S.W.B.Prasetya,J.Hage,A.Elyasov}@uu.nl

Abstract. Testing a web application is typically very complicated. Imposing simple coverage criteria such as function or line coverage is often not sufficient to uncover bugs due to incorrect components integration. Combinatorial testing can enforce a stronger criterion, while still allowing the prioritization of test cases in order to keep the overall effort feasible. Combinatorial testing requires the whole testing domain to be classified and formalized, e.g., in terms of classification trees. At the system testing level, these trees can be quite large. This short paper presents our preliminary work to automatically construct classification trees from loggings of the system, and to subsequently calculate the coverage of our test runs against various combinatorial criteria. We use the tool CTE which allows such criteria to be custom specified. Furthermore, it comes with a graphical interface to simplify the specification of new test sequences.

Keywords: Combinatorial testing · Classification trees · Logging

1 Introduction

A web application typically consists of both client and server components, and is generally quite complex. The server implements complicated business logic, and the client is rich, consisting of a whole range of graphical user interface (GUI) elements that the user can employ. Unit testing is effective for finding bugs in the implementation of the business logic. However, the use of rich clients can easily lead to integration bugs. Unfortunately, the only way to discover such bugs is by testing the application as a whole. Simple event coverage, where we require that every type of GUI event has been tested, is usually too weak [1]. Combinatorial testing, e.g. pair-wise testing, is believed to lead to better results [2]. To systematically perform combinatorial testing, the testing domain should be well-partitioned; a good way to express such a partition is by means of classification trees [3].

T.E.J. Vos, K. Lakhotia, and S. Bauersfeld (Eds.): FITTEST 2013, LNCS 8432, pp. 48–58, 2014.
DOI: 10.1007/978-3-319-07785-7_3, © Springer International Publishing Switzerland 2014

A *classification tree* is the graphical representation of a test specification. It contains the test relevant aspects (e.g. parameters) and their instantiations (e.g. values). In addition to the actual tree, the classification tree method guides the selection of test cases in a combination table. The classification trees of a realistic web application are typically very large. Manually constructing these trees is tedious and error prone. We therefore propose the following research questions:

RQ1: *Can we analyze the system under test (SUT), or its runtime behavior, to acquire elements of the classification trees?*

RQ2: *Can we analyze the SUT to obtain its operational profile?* A software operational profile is a quantitative characterization of the usage of software in the field, e.g. expressed in term of the occurrences probabilities of a set of operations of the software [4]. Such a profile can be used to prioritize testing [5]. In combinatorial testing, we can use profiles to annotate a classification tree.

RQ3: *Can we analyze the SUT to validate, or even to acquire constraints on its valid behavior?*

E.g. when the SUT expects multiple parameters, it is not wise to consider all combinations of these parameters' values as potential test-cases, if it turns out that only few combinations can be considered to be valid. A classification tree can be annotated with such a constraint to prevent such invalid combinations from being tested.

In this paper we describe an approach to automatically construct classification trees from loggings of the application. A log-based approach is chosen because many applications nowadays already employ logging. E.g. web servers produce access logs, embedded software produce operational logs, database servers produce transaction logs, and operating systems produce system logs. Classification trees constructed from the logs are then imported into the CTE XL Professional tool, allowing us to specify combinatorial coverage criterion in CTE XL Professional, and to analyze logs generated by a test suite to see how well it performs on satisfying the criterion. CTE XL Professional also allows constraints to be expressed, so that we can specify more semantically informed context sensitive coverage criteria.

The tooling can also be interesting for supporting exploratory testing [6]. In this approach the tester starts with an abstract testing goal (e.g. to test the user registration feature) and then proceeds to interact with the SUT. As understanding improves, the tester tries to more intelligently interact with the SUT in order to test it with respect to the testing goal. Exploratory testing relies on the tester's cognitive ability to discover which scenarios are more critical, and to focus the testing effort on those. In traditional script-based testing the tester also has to do that, but has to anticipate those scenarios upfront. Moreover, adhering to scripts prohibits the tester from exploring new test cases. By logging exploratory testing sessions, our tooling will help to analyze the combinatorial strength of the testing, and to specify complementary test cases through CTE XL Professional's graphical interface.

2   Concepts

When applying the classification tree method, the first step is to decide which test aspects of the SUT to focus on. For example, the type of user and the type of browser can be two aspects we are interested in. A test aspect can also concerns the SUT's output, or even non-functional aspects such as response time. In the terminology of classification trees, these test aspects are called *classifications*. After selecting relevant test aspects, the tester identifies the (equivalence) *classes* for each classification. The whole process is usually requirements driven. For semantic purposes, and to facilitate structuring, classifications can be (hierarchically) grouped into *compositions*.

Figure 1 contains a classification tree for an example application. The root node *Application* contains the name of the selected SUT. There are two compositions *Inputs* and *Outputs*. Five classifications have been identified: three input (*Param A, Param B, Param C*) and two output classifications (*Result Param A, Result Param B*). For each classification, a set of available classes has been determined, e.g. *Param B* has classes α, β and γ. A *test case* is then constructed by selecting exactly one class for each classification in the tree. E.g. $(a, \alpha, true, \textbf{success}, -1)$ and $(a, \alpha, true, \text{fail}, -1)$ are two test-cases.

Such a test case is "abstract": it cannot be executed yet. To transform it to an executable test. For this, each equivalence class needs to be mapped to a concrete value that represents the class. For example, the classes a, α above may represent negative integers and short strings, respectively, and we may decide to map them to, e.g., -1 and "xyz".

In real world test scenarios, some combinations of classes may actually be invalid. Therefore, constraints may need to be introduced to specify which combinations are allowed. Constraints can be found in many specifications of a software system. They exist for many reasons, such as limitations of the components used in the target system, lack of available resources and even marketing decisions [7]. We use *dependency rules* to formalize constraints [8]. For example we may have a rule that specifies that if *Param A* equals a and *Param B* equals α, then *Param C* may not be *false*. Such a rule is used to annotate classification trees.

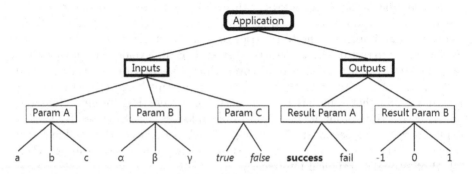

Fig. 1. Classification tree for an example application

A classification tree editor can be used to perform prioritized test case generation [9]. Due to limited test resources, it can be necessary to prioritize and select subsets of test cases. For prioritized test case generation all classes in the tree need to be annotated by weights. The *weight* of a class is its occurrence distribution within the classification to which it belongs. Essentially, this captures the SUT's profile [4], but in terms of classes rather than operations. The assignment of weights to classes requires a data set containing a representative distribution of values and is typically a manual assignment process. In the example from Fig. 1, it might be the case that for *Param A*, its classes *a*, *b*, and *c* occur in 50 %, 40 %, and 10 % of all cases, respectively. Prioritization can be on *usage models* [10], *error models* [11], and *risk models* [12].

The classification tree method can also be used for test sequence generation [13]. The idea is to interpret classification trees as FSMs [14], and then generate covering paths through the FSMs. This involves the identification of allowed transitions between individual classes. In our example, it may be that *Param A* can only be *c* in a test step if there has been an earlier test step with *Param A* equal to *b*. Then *Param A* cannot equal *c* directly after a test step with *a*, but always requires an intermediate step in which it equals *b*.

3   Approach

To answer our research questions, we have implemented a prototype with CTE XL Professional. The prototype requires log files in the FITTEST format [15] from an instrumented SUT. The format is well structured, like XML, which makes interpretation easier; it is more compact than XML to reduce I/O overhead.

3.1   Tool Chain

The algorithm for the construction of the classification tree from logs can be found in Fig. 2. Abstractly, a log is a sequence of entries; each describes the occurrence of an event during operation of the SUT and the state of the SUT after the event. An event description consists of a name, a type and a list of input parameters. While a state is represented by a set of SUT internal variables, which can store complex values such as objects. The logging of object variables produces deeply nested state structure. We view log entries as if they are test steps, together forming a test sequence. The algorithm constructs not only a classification tree, but also a CTE XL test sequence that corresponds to the log. It consists of three phases.

In **phase 1** (Lines1–9), all log entries are parsed. The elements in each log entry are analyzed, and their name and type are stored. The concrete values found during this process are added to the list of possible values for the element. The log entry is then collected together with all contained parameters and their values. The entry's time stamp is also stored.

```
 1: for all log entriesdo
 2:     for all elementsdo
 3:         collect element
 4:         collect type (plain value, array, ...)
 5:         add value to list of values for this element
 6:     end for
 7:     collect entry, set containing parameters and values
 8:     collect time stamp
 9: end for
10: for all types foundddo
11:     create elements in the classification tree
12:     if type is plain variablethen
13:         create classification with that name
14:         for all valuesdo
15:             create class with that value
16:         end for
17:     end if
18:     if type is arraythen
19:         create composition with that name
20:         for all membersdo
21:             create classification with member name
22:             create class 0 (for false, item not contained)
23:             create class 1 (for true, item is contained)
24:         end for
25:     end if
26: end for
27: for all collected entriesdo
28:     create test step
29:     for all plain valuesdo
30:         set mark on corresponding value
31:     end for
32:     for all array elementsdo
33:         set 1 if selected
34:         otherwise 0 (making non-membership explicit)
35:     end for
36:     set time stamp on test step
37: end for
```

Fig. 2. Classification tree construction algorithm

In **phase 2** (Lines 10–26), the classification tree is created. The list of all found elements is processed. If the element is a plain variable, we create a new element of type *classification* in the tree (Line 13). For each possible value of that parameter, a *class* is created (Line 15). Since the values of plain parameters are exclusive, i.e., a single log entry can only contain exactly one value for each parameter, the process maps the variables to classifications and their values to classes.

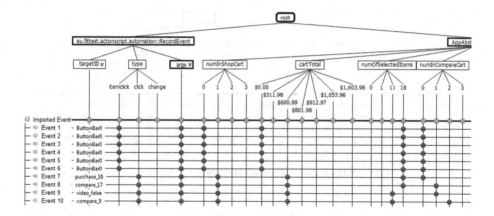

Fig. 3. Classification tree resulting from a log

If the element is an array (with different subsets of members found among the
log entries), we create a new element of type *composition* in the tree (Line 19).
For each array member, we then create a classification (Line 21). For this classification, we always create two classes, 1 and 0 (Lines 22–23). We then use 1
to indicate that the element is a member of the array, and 0 for when it is not.
Since array members are not exclusive, e.g. a log entry can contain arrays with
more than one member, we choose the mapping of members to classifications.
We group them using a parent composition.

In **phase 3** (Lines 27–37), we fill the combination table. Recall that each log
entry is considered as a test step (Line 28). For each plain variable, we select the
corresponding value class from the tree. For arrays, we iterate through all known
possible array elements and compare them against the element of the array from
the current log entry. We select 1-classes for all members contained in the current
entry (Line 33) and 0-classes for absent members (Line 34). Finally, we set the
relative time stamp on the test step (Line 36).

The result from an example import is shown in Fig. 3.

The left branch of the tree contains details about the events of an application.
The classification *targetID* has been collapsed to save space and its selected
values are given as text in the test matrix. The classification *type* is a typical
example of a plain value variable: it consists of three classes *itemclick*, *click*
and *change*. As can be seen from the test matrix, whenever the *targetID* is
ButtonBar0, the corresponding event *type* is *itemclick* (Events 1–6). Elements
with a different *targetID* cause events of *type click* instead. The event *type change*
is not contained in the first 10 events.

The composition *args* was collapsed in Fig. 3 in order to save space. Details
are given in Fig. 4.

For each member of the array *args*, a classification has been created in the
tree. In this case, there are twelve different possible array members. The values that occur in a particular event are those that select 1 for that event.

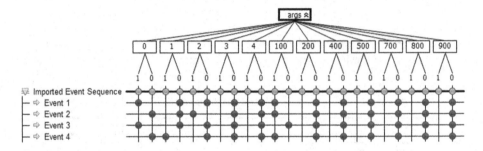

Fig. 4. Classification tree part for array

For example, for event 1 these are 0 and 100, and for event 2 there are 2 and 100. An empty array would also be a possible configuration and would feature all zeros selected.

3.2   Addressing the RQs

Earlier in the paper, we posed three research questions. Below we discuss our progress in addressing these questions with a log-based approach towards answering these questions, and challenges that are still left for future work.

RQ1: *Can logs be used to acquire elements of classification trees?*

Since logs already contain repeating similarities which give some hints of the structures that underlie the SUT, the identification of *classifications* is quite straightforward; moreover, these also help in identifying missing test aspects in the test specification. To construct the *classes* of the classifications, we took a direct approach where we map each occurring concrete parameter value to its own class. Therefore, the resulting classification tree may be too verbose. Ideally, we would want to merge different parameter values that result in the same behavior into the same equivalence class. This remains future work. The expected challenge here is the issue of over and under-approximation [16]. Furthermore, for general automatic construction of classification trees, or any kind of test specifications in general, the scalability and applicability highly depend on the granularity, and the general quality of used logs. This leads to the question how to get such logs in the first place.

RQ2: *Can logs be used to assess profiles of the application under test?*

The calculation of the classes' distributions is a simple task. It involves counting all events in the logs and then calculating the ratio of each class occurrence in the logs to the total number of events. This helps testers to quickly obtain an estimation of the class weights from the observed distribution.

Calculation of error probabilities [11] is future work. The error probability of a class is the probability that an error occurs when this class is used in a test case. In principle, this can be done by comparing values in the logs that represent the SUT's state or outputs to their expected values. If they do not match, one could assume the execution that produced the value to be erroneous.

The error probability would then be the ratio of erroneous executions against all executions. However, this requires oracles to be specified and integrated into the tool, which we have not done yet.

RQ3: *Can logs be used to validate existing and acquire new constraints?*

The classification tree editor is already capable of checking a test case against a set of behavior constraints in the form of dependency rules [8]. Since in our approach logs are transformed into test sequences, they can thus be used to check the validity of existing dependency rules. If there is a mismatch, then either the system is not behaving correctly or there is a problem with the test specification.

Given a long enough execution time or a high number of repetitions of the actual system one may assume that all combinations that did not occur can be considered invalid. This allows the automatic extraction of dependency rules from the logs. A potential problem is, again, over and under-approximation. If the execution time is too short, too many combinations are considered forbidden. We think this RQ can only be solved partially, and it still requires future work.

To identify transitions between classes of the classification tree, it is necessary to identify individual test steps from the logs. By monitoring the order in which classes occur, one can start from the assumption that sequences of any two classes that occur indicate a valid transition between these two classes. However, classes that do not occur in a certain order do not necessarily indicate an invalid transition. The quality of the identification is strongly dependent on the extent that the logs are representative of the system's behavior. Future work is still required.

4   Related Work

Previous work to automatically generate and validate classification trees, e.g., using Z-specifications, includes [17,18]. However, the requirement to first have a formal Z specification may in practice be unrealistic. A log-based approach is more pragmatic, since many modern applications already employ logging.

Logs can potentially provide much information; if semantic information can be extracted, powerful analyses become possible. For example, logs can be converted into a different representation to be queried for properties. Database-style and Prolog-style queries have been investigated in this context [19,20]. It may be worthwhile to investigate the facilitation of querying elements of a classification tree against the logs. Marchetto et al. [21] and Lorenzoli et al. [22] investigated how FSMs (modeling the behavior of a program) can be reconstructed from logs. Nguyen et al. investigated how classification trees can be generated from FSMs [23]. However, a tree in Nguyen et al. represents a family of test sequences through an FSM, whereas our tree represents the classification of the entire SUT. Their choice is natural when the goal is to optimize the combinatorial coverage of each test sequence, whereas ours is natural to measure and optimize the combinatorial coverage of an entire suite.

In practice people often use a "simple" log format, e.g. the Common Log Format produced by many webservers. Logs produced using the popular log4j family of logging libraries also employ a simple format. Such a format allows log entries to be accompanied with free style text. When these free text fields are used, they often contain useful semantic information. Extracting or even classifying the semantical information from the free text is a difficult problem. Jain et al. [24] applied clustering techniques to automatically classify unstructured log messages. The clustering is based on common textual structures within the messages, which are then associated to some semantic categorization of the messages including info-messages and (various kinds of) alert-messages. If we can assume to work with more rigidly formatted logs, e.g. in Daikon format [25] or FITTEST format [15], the clustering approach can potentially be lifted to identify equivalence classes from the semantic parts of the log entries. This in turn may be useful for the inference of more abstract classes in the inferred classification trees.

5   Conclusion and Future Work

We have presented the use of logs for the generation, completion and validation of classification trees. We have proposed three research questions and discussed possible solutions, outcomes, and future work. A working prototype has been developed and integrated into CTE XL Professional. The answers we found for the research questions are promising:

- For **RQ1,** we found out that elements of the classification tree can indeed be acquired from logs. We do, however, only obtain concrete values from log and a mapping to abstract values is not provided. Some future work is still required for grouping into equivalence classes.
- For **RQ2,** we are able to calculate occurrence probabilities, though the calculation of error probabilities still has some issues.
- For **RQ3,** the validation of logs against dependency rules has been performed successfully. The acquisition of dependency rules and allowed transitions depends on the amount of logs available.

Providing positive answers to our **RQs** helps to improve the quality of test design. Reducing manual labor when creating test specifications in terms of classification trees helps test engineers to focus on the actual product features and changes.

While all work has been done on classification trees we are certain that results can be extended to other test specification formats as well.

We have earlier indicated what challenges are left for future work. Additionally, we want to perform a large scale evaluation.

Acknowledgment. This work is supported by EU grant ICT-257574 (FITTEST).

References

1. Memon, A.M., Soffa, M.L., Pollack, M.E.: Coverage criteria for GUI testing. In: Proceedings of the 8th European Software Engineering Conference Held Jointly with 9th ACM SIGSOFT International Symposium on Foundations of Software Engineering, ESEC/FSE-9, pp. 256–267. ACM, New York (2001)
2. Nie, C., Leung, H.: A survey of combinatorial testing. ACM Comput. Surv. **43**, 11:1–11:29 (2011)
3. Grochtmann, M., Grimm, K.: Classification trees for partition testing. Softw. Test. Verif. Reliab. **3**(2), 63–82 (1993)
4. Musa, J.D.: Operational profiles in software-reliability engineering. IEEE Softw. **10**(2), 14–32 (1993)
5. Misra, R.B., Saravana Kumar, K.: Software operational profile based test case allocation using fuzzy logic. Int. J. Autom. Comput. **4**(4), 388 (2007)
6. Bach, J.: Exploratory testing explained (2003). http://www.satisfice.com/articles/et-article.pdf
7. Cohen, M.B., Dwyer, M.B., Shi, J.: Interaction testing of highly-configurable systems in the presence of constraints. In: ISSTA '07: Proceedings of the 2007 International Symposium on Software Testing and Analysis, New York, NY, USA, pp. 129–139 (2007)
8. Lehmann, E., Wegener, J.: Test case design by means of the CTE XL. In: Proceedings of the 8th European International Conference on Software Testing, Analysis and Review (EuroSTAR 2000), Kopenhagen, Denmark, December 2000
9. Kruse, P.M., Luniak, M.: Automated test case generation using classification trees. Softw. Qual. Prof. **13**(1), 4–12 (2010)
10. Walton, G.H., Poore, J.H., Trammell, C.J.: Statistical testing of software based on a usage model. Softw. Pract. Exper. **25**(1), 97–108 (1995)
11. Elbaum, S., Malishevsky, A.G., Rothermel, G.: Test case prioritization: a family of empirical studies. IEEE Trans. Softw. Eng. **28**(2), 159–182 (2002)
12. Amland, S.: Risk-based testing: risk analysis fundamentals and metrics for software testing including a financial application case study. J. Syst. Softw. **53**(3), 287–295 (2000)
13. Kruse, P.M., Wegener, J.: Test sequence generation from classification trees. In: Proceedings of ICST 2012 Workshops (ICSTW 2012), Montreal, Canada (2012)
14. Conrad, M., Drr, H., Fey, I., Yap, A.: Model-based generation and structured representation of test scenarios. In: Proceedings of the Workshop on Software-Embedded Systems Testing, Gaithersburg, Maryland, USA (1999)
15. Prasetya, I.S.W.B., Middelkoop, A., Elyasov, A., Hage, J.: D6.1: FITTEST Logging Approach, Project no. 257574, FITTEST Future Internet Testing (2011)
16. Tonella, P., Marchetto, A., Nguyen, D.C., Jia, Y., Lakhotia, K., Harman, M.: Finding the optimal balance between over and under approximation of models inferred from execution logs. In: 2012 IEEE 5th International Conference on Software Testing, Verification and Validation, pp. 21–30. IEEE (2012)
17. Singh, H., Conrad, M., Sadeghipour, S.: Test case design based on Z and the classification-tree method. In: Proceedings of the 1st International Conference on Formal Engineering Methods, ICFEM '97, pp. 81–90. IEEE Computer Society, Washington, DC (1997)
18. Hierons, R.M., Harman, M.: Automatically generating information from a Z specification to support the classification tree method. In: Bert, D., Bowen, J.P., King, S., Waldén, M. (eds.) ZB 2003. LNCS, vol. 2651, pp. 388–407. Springer, Heidelberg (2003)

19. Feather, M.S.: Rapid application of lightweight formal methods for consistency analyses. IEEE Trans. Softw. Eng. **24**(11), 949–959 (1998)
20. Ducasse, S., Girba, T., Wuyts, R.: Object-oriented legacy system trace-based logic testing. In: 10th European Conference on Software Maintenance and Reengineering (CSMR). IEEE (2006)
21. Marchetto, A., Tonella, P., Ricca, F.: State-based testing of Ajax web applications. In: ICST, pp. 121–130. IEEE (2008)
22. Lorenzoli, D., Mariani, L., Pezzè, M.: Automatic generation of software behavioral models. In: 30th International Conference on Software Engineering, pp. 501–510. ACM (2008)
23. Nguyen, C.D., Marchetto, A., Tonella, P.: Combining model-based and combinatorial testing for effective test case generation. In: Proceedings of International Symposium on Software Testing and Analysis (ISSTA), Minneapolis, Minnesota, USA (2012)
24. Jain, S., Singh, I., Chandra, A., Zhang, Z.-L., Bronevetsky, G.: Extracting the textual and temporal structure of supercomputing logs. In: Yang, Y., Parashar, M., Muralidhar, R., Prasanna, V.K. (eds.) HiPC, pp. 254–263. IEEE (2009)
25. Ernst, M.D., Perkins, J.H., Guo, P.J., McCamant, S., Pacheco, C., Tschantz, M.S., Xiao, C.: The Daikon system for dynamic detection of likely invariants. Sci. Comput. Program. **69**(1–3), 35–45 (2007)

N-Gram Based Test Sequence Generation from Finite State Models

Paolo Tonella[✉], Roberto Tiella, and Cu D. Nguyen

Software Engineering Research Unit, Fondazione Bruno Kessler, Trento, Italy
{tonella,tiella,cunduy}@fbk.eu
http://se.fbk.eu

Abstract. Model based testing offers a powerful mechanism to test applications that change dynamically and continuously, for which only some limited black-box knowledge is available (this is typically the case of future internet applications). Models can be inferred from observations of real executions and test cases can be derived from models, according to various strategies (e.g., graph or random visits). The problem is that a relatively large proportion of the test cases obtained in this way might result to be non executable, because they involve infeasible paths.

In this paper, we propose a novel test case derivation strategy, based on the computation of the N-gram statistics. Event sequences are generated for which the subsequences of size N respect the distribution of the N-tuples observed in the execution traces. In this way, generated and observed sequences share the same context (up to length N), hence increasing the likelihood for the generated ones of being actually executable. A consequence of the increased proportion of feasible test cases is that model coverage is also expected to increase.

1 Introduction

In model based testing, finite state machines present models of the application under test which support the derivation of test cases [1]. The underlying idea is that the model encodes all relevant application behaviours and abstracts away the irrelevant implementation details, so that testing can be focused on covering all critical application behaviours, without wasting time on non-critical features of the application. Model based testing does not require white box knowledge of the application under test. Moreover, incremental model update algorithms [2] can be used with continuously and autonomously changing applications, as future internet applications.

Models can be defined upfront, at design time, but such practice is not very common and is costly due to labour work. Alternatively, models can be inferred from observations of actual executions, recorded as log traces. The two main techniques for model inference from execution traces are state abstraction and event sequence abstraction. In state abstraction, abstraction functions are defined to map concrete states into abstract states, so as to control the size of the inferred model and to allow for generalisation from the actually observed

T.E.J. Vos, K. Lakhotia, and S. Bauersfeld (Eds.): FITTEST 2013, LNCS 8432, pp. 59–74, 2014.
DOI: 10.1007/978-3-319-07785-7_4, © Springer International Publishing Switzerland 2014

states [3]. Event sequence abstraction takes advantage of regular language inference algorithms, such as k-tail [4], or its variants [5,6]. A finite state machine is obtained which recognises the language of the event sequences observed in execution logs. Such finite state machines are actually a generalisation of the observed sequences (not just their union).

The generalisation performed by model inference is usually *unsound*, which means the inferred models might introduce infeasible behaviours (paths allowed in the model that are impossible in the real application), hence over-generalising, and they might exclude some possible behaviours (paths allowed in the real application that do not exist in the model), hence under-generalising [7]. While the latter problem can be tackled by increasing the number and the representativeness of the execution traces used during model inference, so as to make sure the model includes as many behaviours as possible, the former problem is difficult to overcome and is particularly troublesome for testers. In fact, during test sequence generation an over-generalising model might produce test cases that traverse infeasible event sequences. For the tester, proving that a given test case derived from the model is associated with an infeasible path is a quite difficult task. In the general case, the problem is undecidable [8]. While particularly severe with inferred models, the presence of infeasible paths that cannot be tested is also a major problem with manually defined models.

In this work, we investigate a test sequence derivation strategy based on the notion of N-grams [9], which aims at mitigating the problem of the generation of infeasible paths. The idea is that, during the generation of a test sequence, the next event to add to the sequence should be selected according to the probability of the N-grams, as observed in the corpus of training traces. By constructing test sequences as concatenations of N-grams, inserted according to the observed frequency of occurrence, we expect to reduce dramatically the generation of infeasible test sequences. Our preliminary results on two applications confirm this speculation. Moreover, in comparison with other strategies (e.g., graph visit or random generation), N-gram based test sequence generation exploits some context information (the previous $N-1$ events in the sequence) to determine the probability of occurrence of the next event, according to the actual sequences recorded in the execution logs. By reducing the number of infeasible sequences, N-gram based test sequence derivation delivers several benefits to testers: (1) the manual effort to confirm that some test sequences are infeasible is reduced; (2) coverage is increased, since a higher number of test sequences can be enacted and executed during testing; (3) the test case concretisation effort (necessary to supply concrete input data and the surrounding test harness) is also reduced, since less effort is wasted on infeasible cases.

The paper is organised as follows: Sect. 2 provides some background on model based testing and on the most widely used test sequence derivation strategies (namely, graph visit and random generation). Our novel technique for N-gram based test case derivation is presented in Sect. 3. Empirical data comparing our approach with graph visit and random generation are provided in Sect. 4. Related works (Sect. 5) are followed by conclusions and future work (Sect. 6).

2   Baseline Sequence Generation Strategies in Model Based Testing

Model-based testing is an approach to generate test cases using a model of the application under test [10]. Dias Neto et al. [1] and Shafique [11] surveyed the state of the art in model-based testing. A model that describes structure and behaviour of the SUT is useful to acquire the knowledge needed to generate effective test cases. The model, in fact, provides an abstract and concise view of the application by focusing on specific aspects, i.e., classes of application behaviours associated with different application states. One of the most frequently used kinds of model is the Finite State Machine (FSM) model, even though some alternatives do exist (e.g., Briand et al. [12] use UML class and sequence diagrams). A node in the FSM represents a state of the application and it can be determined by, e.g., the values of class attributes (in case of object-oriented applications [13,14]) or the values of graphical objects (in case of GUI-based applications [15–17]). FSMs are named *concrete* if each FSM state represents an actual application state or *abstract* if each FSM state represents a set (i.e., an equivalence class) of concrete states (e.g., [16,18]). A transition in the FSM represents an application event/action (e.g., a method call, an event handler invocation) that can change the application state, if executed. Additionally, guards and conditions can enrich the model to capture the context in which events and actions are executed.

FSM models are exploited to generate test cases. By traversing the application FSM, sequences of application events can be extracted, so as to satisfy given coverage criteria [13]. For example, state or transition coverage (every FSM state or transition needs to be exercised by at least one test case) are often used, even if domain-specific (e.g., semantically interacting events [15]) criteria are sometimes preferred. As examples of output test sequences, based on the model presented in Fig. 1 we can extract the following test sequences: $\langle e_1, e_2 \rangle, \langle e_1, e_2, e_3 \rangle, \langle e_4, e_5, e_3 \rangle$.

Different test case derivation strategies can be used to produce a set of test cases that satisfies the adequacy criterion of choice (e.g., transition coverage). Graph visit and random model traversal are among the most widely used strategies. We describe them in the next two subsections.

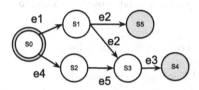

Fig. 1. An example of a model in FSM format; S_0 is the initial node, S_4 and S_5 are final nodes.

2.1   Graph Visit

Depth-first and breadth-first model traversal can be used to derive test sequences from the model, interpreted as a directed graph. Figure 2 shows the pseudocode of the depth first test sequence generation strategy (DFV: Depth First Visit). Procedure *depthFirstVisit* determines the set of successor nodes that have not been visited yet (set *next*, where notation m^e indicates that m is a successor node if event e is triggered). Each of them is randomly chosen and the graph visit is recursively activated on such node, if the associated transition has remained yet to be visited (in fact, a previous recursive call of *depthFirstVisit* might have changed its visited state). This node is concatenated to the path traversed so far during the visit ($p + s^e$). When no unexplored successor node is found (*next* is empty), the visit terminates and the traversed path is added to the test suite being generated. The depth first visit procedure is called multiple times from the start node, until some adequacy criterion is satisfied (by construction, when the adequacy criterion is transition coverage, *depthFirstVisit* will be called just once). The global hash table *visited* records whether each transition has been visited or not during the sequence generation (it is reset inside the main loop, before calling *depthFirstVisit*). The result of this procedure is non deterministic, since it depends on the successor node s^e chosen for the continuation of the visit. Different choices may result in transitions being covered at different times during the visit, which in turn might give raise to different test sequences being added to the final test suite.

```
proc depthFirstVisit(n : Node, p : Path)  ≡
    do
        next := {m^e ∈ succ[n] | ¬visited[⟨n, m⟩_e]};
        if (¬empty(next))
            then
                while (¬empty(next)) do
                    s^e := randChoose(next);
                    if (¬visited[⟨n, s⟩_e])
                        then
                            visited[⟨n, s⟩_e] := true;
                            depthFirstVisit(s^e, p + s^e);
                    fi
                    next := remove(next, s^e);
                od
            else
                if (p increases adequacy) then addToTestSuite(p);  fi
        fi
    od.
while adequacy criterion not satisfied do
        visited := ∅
        p := depthFirstVisit(startNode, ⟨⟩);
od
```

Fig. 2. Test sequence derivation by depth first visit

```
proc breadthFirstVisit(n : Node, p : Path)  ≡
  do
       end := true;
       next := {mᵉ ∈ succ[n] |  ¬visited[⟨n, m⟩ₑ]};
       while (¬empty(next)) do
              end := false;
              sᵉ := randChoose(next);
              visited[⟨n, s⟩ₑ] := true;
              addToFifoQueue(Q, p + sᵉ);
              next := remove(next, sᵉ);
       od
       if (end ∧ p increases adequacy) then addToTestSuite(p);  fi
       if (¬emptyFifoQueue(Q))
          then
                  p = getFromFifoQueue(Q);
                  breadthFirstVisit(last(p), p);
       fi
  od.
  while adequacy criterion not satisfied do
          visited := ∅
          p := breadthFirstVisit(startNode, ⟨⟩);
  od
```

Fig. 3. Test sequence derivation by breadth first visit

Figure 3 shows the pseudocode of the breadth first test sequence generation strategy (BFV: Breadth First Visit). Procedure *breadthFirstVisit* uses a global queue data structure (Q) to store the partially explored paths to be considered later during the visit. All unexplored successor nodes (set *next*) are concatenated to the current traversal path p and are added to Q for future exploration. When no unexplored successor node exists, the visit terminates and the traversed path p is added to the test suite. If queue Q is not empty, there are some pending paths that need to be traversed through recursive invocation of *breadthFirstVisit*. This procedure involves some degree of non-determinism, related to the order in which the paths to be explored are added to Q. In fact, different orders will change the *visited* state of transitions at different times, possibly resulting in different test sequences being added to the final test suite. This is accounted for by the random selection of the node s^e from set *next*, when $p + s^e$ is added to Q. Transition coverage is guaranteed by BFV by construction. An adequacy criterion different from transition coverage (e.g., maximum test budget) may require multiple invocations of procedure *breadthFirstVisit*.

2.2 Random Visit

Figure 4 shows the pseudocode of the random test sequence generation strategy (RAND: Random visit). Procedure *randomVisit* decides whether to add another event to the current test sequence or not in a stochastic way. With probability

```
proc randomVisit(n : Node, p : Path)  ≡
  do
    if (randProb() ≤ RECURSE_PROB ∧ succ[n] ≠ ∅)
      then
        sᵉ := randChoose(succ[n]);
        p := randomVisit(s, p + sᵉ);
    fi
    if (p increases adequacy) then addToTestSuite(p);  fi
  od.
while adequacy criterion not satisfied do
    p := randomVisit(startNode, ⟨⟩);
od
```

Fig. 4. Test sequence derivation by random visit

$RECURSE\_PROB$, a randomly selected successor of the current node is added to the current event sequence and *randomVisit* is invoked recursively. When recursion is not activated, the generated test sequence is added to the test suite, if it increases the test suite adequacy level. Multiple random visits are performed, until the adequacy criterion (e.g., transition coverage) is satisfied.

The algorithm is clearly non deterministic. The algorithm parameter $RECURSE\_PROB$ determines the length of the generated event sequences. To produce event sequences with an average length equal to that observed in the execution traces, $RECURSE\_PROB$ can be set to $AVG\_TRC\_SZ/(1+AVG\_TRC\_SZ)$, where AVG_TRC_SZ is the average length of the logged event sequences.

3   N-Gram Based Test Sequence Derivation

N-gram language models are widely used in Natural Language Processing (NLP) [9]. A N-gram language model is a probabilistic language model where the probability that a word (an event in our case) e is preceded by a sequence of words (events) depends only on the last $N - 1$ words.

For example, given a training corpus of English sentences and N equals to 2 (bi-gram), the probability that the word "the" appears after the sentence "she is so beautiful that" is approximated with the probability that "the" follows "that".

Using probabilistic models, knowledge about the N-gram statistics supports *word prediction*. In turn, word prediction is a key component used to address several NLP tasks, such as speech recognition, handwriting recognition, machine translation, spell correction, natural language generation, etc. In fact, NLP algorithms usually admit multiple sentence derivations and N-gram statistics can be used to select the most likely among the possible derivations.

The problem with model based test sequence generation is somewhat similar. Among all possible event sequences that satisfy some adequacy criterion (e.g., transition coverage), only a subset represent *feasible* event sequences, i.e.,

```
proc ngramVisit(n : Node, p : Path)  ≡
   do
      if (randProb() ≤ RECURSE_PROB)
         then
            sᵉ := ngramChoose(succ[n], suffix(p, N − 1));
            p := ngramVisit(s, p + sᵉ);
      fi
      if (p increases adequacy) then addToTestSuite(p);  fi
   od.
while adequacy criterion not satisfied do
      p := ngramVisit(startNode, ⟨⟩);
od
```

Fig. 5. Test sequence derivation by N-gram probability

event sequences that can be actually executed against the application under test. Infeasible sequences involve execution steps whose order is forbidden by the application under test or events whose valid inputs prevents the execution of a later subsequence. Avoiding the generation of infeasible event sequences is very similar to avoiding the derivation of unlikely sentences and N-gram statistics can be used in a similar way as in NLP to achieve such purpose. In fact, by generating event sequences that contain N-grams previously observed in real executions we increase the likelihood that such sequences will in turn be executable.

Figure 5 shows the pseudocode of the N-gram test sequence generation strategy (by NGRAM2, NGRAM3, etc., we indicate that N, the size of the tuples considered in the N-gram statistics, is respectively 2, 3, etc.). The procedure is similar to the random visit shown in Fig. 4, the key difference being the way in which the next event to add to the event sequence is chosen. Instead of choosing which successor node to add randomly (i.e., according to a uniform probability distribution), the successor to add is chosen in accordance with the conditioned probabilities of the next events given the last $N − 1$ events in the current path p:

$$ngramChoose(S, \langle e_1, \ldots, e_{N-1} \rangle) := s^e \in S \quad with \ prob. \ P(e \mid e_1, \ldots, e_{N-1})$$

The conditioned probabilities $P(e \mid e_1, \ldots, e_{N-1})$ are estimated from the frequency of occurrence of the N-tuples $\langle e^{(1)}, e_1, \ldots, e_{N-1} \rangle, \ldots, \langle e^{(k)}, e_1, \ldots, e_{N-1} \rangle$ in the execution logs. Specifically, the choice (among $e^{(1)}, \ldots, e^{(k)}$) of the next event to add to the event sequence has a probability which is proportional to the frequency of occurrence of the respective tuples ($\langle e^{(1)}, e_1, \ldots, e_{N-1} \rangle, \ldots, \langle e^{(k)}, e_1, \ldots, e_{N-1} \rangle$).

When no N-tuple $\langle e, e_1, \ldots, e_{N-1} \rangle$ appears in the available execution traces, the next event e is selected randomly among the possible transitions outgoing from the current node n. In such cases the NGRAM strategy degenerates to the random strategy. This is expected to occur at increased frequency when N takes higher and higher values, since only a small fraction of the possible N-tuples will be represented in the observed traces. We can thus predict that the performance of NGRAM will converge to the performance of RAND as the value of the parameter N increases.

4   Case Studies

We have conducted two case studies to answer the following research questions:

- **RQ1 (Feasibility):** How many feasible test sequences are generated by the N-gram strategy, as compared to the graph visit and the random strategies?
- **RQ2 (Coverage):** What level of transition coverage is achieved by the N-gram strategy, as compared to the graph visit and the random strategies?
- **RQ3 (Test suite size):** Are test sequences generated by the N-gram strategy longer than those generated by the graph visit and the random strategies?
- **RQ4 (Test case length):** Is the length of the test sequences generated by the N-gram strategy greater than the length of test sequences generated by the graph visit and the random strategies?

The first two research questions are key to validate the proposed approach. We conjecture that N-gram based test sequence generation will produce fewer infeasible test sequences (hence, higher coverage) than graph visit or random model traversal. With these two research questions we want to empirically assess whether our conjecture is confirmed or not by the experimental data.

The last two research questions deal with some interesting properties of the automatically generated test suites, namely, the number of test sequences they contain and their length. To make the comparison fair, we adopt the same adequacy criterion with all alternative test sequence generation strategies: transition coverage. All test suites produced by the various strategies will be transition coverage adequate and will contain only test cases that contribute to increasing such adequacy level.

4.1   Metrics

To address the four research questions listed above, we have collected the following metrics:

- **FEAS (RQ1):** Ratio between feasible test sequences and total number of test sequences generated by each test strategy.
- **COV (RQ2):** Ratio between covered transitions and total number of transitions in the model.
- **SZ (RQ3):** Number of test sequences in the test suite.
- **LEN (RQ4):** Average number of events in each test sequence of the test suite.

While metrics COV, SZ and LEN can be easily measured automatically, using tools, metric FEAS requires human judgment, since it is not possible to automatically decide if a test sequence is feasible (i.e., whether it can be executed

Table 1. Abstraction functions used to infer the model of Flexstore

State	Abstraction
$n1$	[initial] *false*
$n2$	$s1 = 0 \wedge s2 = 0 \wedge s3 > 0$
$n3$	$s1 = 0 \wedge s2 = 0 \wedge s3 = 0$
$n4$	$s1 > 0 \wedge s2 = 0 \wedge s3 > 0$
$n5$	$s1 > 0 \wedge s2 = 0 \wedge s3 = 0$
$n6$	$s1 > 0 \wedge s2 > 0 \wedge s3 > 0$
$n7$	$s1 > 0 \wedge s2 > 0 \wedge s3 = 0$
$n8$	$s1 = 0 \wedge s2 > 0 \wedge s3 > 0$
$n9$	$s1 = 0 \wedge s2 > 0 \wedge s3 = 0$
$s1$	numInShopCart
$s2$	numInCompareCart
$s3$	numOfSelectedItems

by providing proper input data) or not (the problem is undecidable in the general case). We manually defined the set of constraints for the subject applications to characterise the event sequences that can be legally submitted to and executed by the system under test.

4.2 Subjects

The applications under test are Flexstore and Cyclos. Flexstore[1] is an on-line shopping application developed by Adobe and made available from the company's web site to demonstrate the capabilities of their testing framework. It is a client-side application developed in Flex and run by the Flash plug-in accounting for about 3.5k LOC (line of code). The application allows the user to browse a catalog of mobile phones and to focus on a subset of models by means of filters, such as price range, camera, tri-band, and video availability. The customer can select one or more models to perform comparisons among features. Eventually, the customer can put one or more phones in their shopping cart.

Cyclos[2] is a popular open source Java/Servlet Web Application, supporting e-commerce and banking, accounting for about 75k LOC. Its main features include: banking (e.g., payments, loans, brokering), e-commerce (e.g., advertising, member payments) and many others (e.g., access control, management). Cyclos is a quite large system. In our experiment we focused only on the payment feature of Cyclos.

We have obtained execution traces for both applications by navigating and exercising the various application features, according to a high level functional coverage criterion: all functionalities provided in the application menus have been executed with input data that a user would be typically expected to provide. The two applications have been instrumented so as to support trace collection.

---

[1] http://www.adobe.com/devnet/flex/samples/flex_store_v2.html
[2] http://project.cyclos.org

Table 2. Abstraction functions used to infer the model of Cyclos

State	Abstraction
$n1$	[initial] $false$
$n2$	$s1 = true \land s2 = true$
$n3$	$s3 = null \land s4 = null \land s5 \neq null \land s6 = null \land s7 = null \land s8 = 0$
$n4$	$s3 = null \land s4 = null \land s5 \neq null \land s6 = null \land s7 \neq null \land s8 = 0$
$n5$	$s9 = true$
$n6$	$s3 = null \land s4 = null \land s5 \neq null \land s6 = null \land s7 \neq null \land s8 > 0$
$n7$	$s3 = null \land s4 = null \land s5 \neq null \land s6 \neq null \land s7 = null \land s8 = 0$
$s1$	LoggedIn
$s2$	PaymentReady
$s3$	typeRow
$s4$	customValuesRow
$s5$	trSchedulingType
$s6$	scheduling_singlePayment
$s7$	scheduling_multiplePayments
$s8$	paymentCounts
$s9$	End

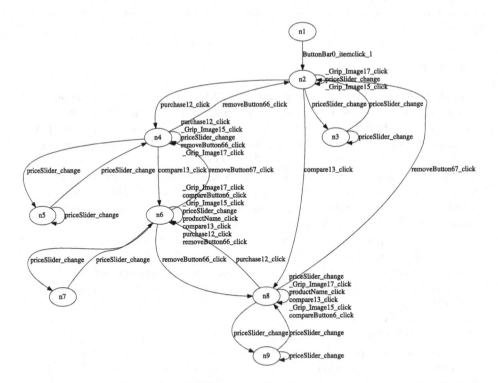

Fig. 6. Finite state model of Flexstore

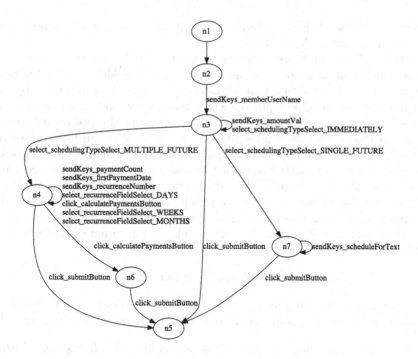

Fig. 7. Finite state model of Cyclos

We collected 100 traces for Flexstore and 999 traces for Cyclos. In total, 3,000 events have been executed in Flexstore during trace production, while 5,965 events have been executed in Cyclos.

We have obtained a FSM model of each application by applying state-based abstraction to the execution traces. Specifically, we have used the model inference component [16] of the FITTEST[3] Integrated Testing Environment (ITE). The state abstraction functions used for model inference with Flexstore and Cyclos are shown respectively in Tables 1 and 2 (state variables are mapped to application variables at the bottom of each table). The resulting FSM models are shown in Figs. 6 and 7.

4.3   Procedure

The test sequence generation algorithms DFV, BFV, RAND and NGRAM, whose pseudocode is shown in Figs. 2, 3, 4, and 5, have been applied to the models inferred for Flexstore and Cyclos (shown in Figs. 6 and 7). NGRAM has been applied with N = 2, 3, 4, using the same traces used for model inference to obtain the N-gram statistics needed by the algorithm. Since all these algorithms are non deterministic, each of them has been run 100 times. Results are averaged over the 100 runs. In all runs, each algorithm was executed with transition

---

[3] EU FP7 project n. 257574.

coverage set as the adequacy criterion to satisfy (of course not all test sequences generated from the model are feasible).

Metrics SZ and LEN are obtained by measuring the number of test cases and the number of events per test case in each test suite. Metrics COV has been obtained by means of a tool that visits the FSM models of the two applications based on the feasible input sequences in each test suite, keeping track of the covered transitions. Metrics FEAS has been measured based on two sets of constraints that define the legal sequences of actions that can be executed on the two applications. Test cases which contain event sequences violating such constraints have been marked as infeasible and have been subtracted from the count of the feasible sequences. They also do not contribute to metrics COV.

Feasibility constraints have the form: $[g]e$, indicating that event e can be triggered only if the guard condition g is true; otherwise, the event sequence being executed is deemed infeasible. An example of a constraint manually defined for Flexstore is the following:

$$[numOfSelectedItems > 0]compare13\_click$$

indicating that event *compare13_click* can be triggered only in a state where *numOfSelectedItems* is greater than zero. For Cyclos, an example of constraint is:

$$[amount > 0 \wedge (immediate \vee single) \vee (multiple \wedge count > 0)]click\_submitButton$$

It is possible to submit a payment if the amount is greater than zero and the payment is immediate or single. Multiple payments require in addition that the recurrence count is greater than zero.

4.4   Results

The results of the experiment are shown in Tables 3 and 4. Let us consider the graph visit and random strategies first. On Flexstore, BFV achieved a relatively high feasibility and coverage score, while the other strategies performed

Table 3. Results obtained for the Flexstore case study. Techniques (on rows) are compared in terms of feasibility, model coverage, TS size and TC length. Best values are in boldface. For them p-values are at the bottom.

	FEAS	COV	SZ	LEN
DFV	0.02	0.11	4.74	25.34
BFV	**0.72**	**0.65**	34.00	3.38
RAND	0.04	0.27	4.26	55.01
NGRAM2	0.39	0.78	4.81	47.73
NGRAM3	**0.57**	**0.81**	4.96	49.66
NGRAM4	0.46	0.71	5.07	45.48

p-value(BFV, NGRAM3, FEAS) = 1.793e-09
p-value(NGRAM3, BFV, COV) < 2.2e-16

substantially worse. On Cyclos, BFV achieved comparatively higher feasibility, while on coverage DFV, BFV and RAND performed roughly the same.

On both applications, the NGRAM based approach was superior to the other strategies in terms of both feasibility and coverage. On Flexstore the best performance was achieved by NGRAM3, while on Cyclos it was achieved by NGRAM2. On Flexstore, the absolute difference of the best (NGRAM3) COV values with respect to BFV is substantial (0.16) and statistically significant (very low p-values), according to the Wilcoxon test. BFV has higher FEAS than NGRAM3 because it tends to generate many (34 per test suite) short (3.38 events per test case) test sequences, which are feasible, but cover the model transitions less than the longer NGRAM3 test sequences. On Cyclos, the difference between NGRAM2 and BFV/DFV on both FEAS and COV is substantial (0.36 and 0.20) and statistically significant.

On Cyclos, NGRAM2 has the best performance in terms of feasibility. NGRAM2 achieved the maximum possible FEAS score (1.0), as in this application bi-grams subsume the feasibility constraints. Coverage also reached the maximum possible value, since two transitions in the model are infeasible, which makes the maximum achievable coverage equal to 0.94. With tri-grams (NGRAM3) several bi-gram constraints are still met, but there are cases where no tri-gram is applicable (because there is no such triple in the collected execution traces), which results in a random selection of the next event. FEAS and COV are correspondingly higher with NGRAM2, but COV is still quite high with NGRAM3. It can be noticed that in both applications as N increases (from 2 to 3 and 4) the performance of the N-gram based methods tends to converge to that of random, both in terms of FEAS and COV, as expected.

In summary, we can positively answer RQ1 and RQ2: *N-gram based test sequence generation produces a higher proportion of feasible event sequences and achieves higher coverage than graph visit or random approaches.*

In terms of test suite size and test case length (RQ3, RQ4), we can notice that BFV produced test suites with a lot of very short test cases (34/14 test

Table 4. Results obtained for the Cyclos case study. Techniques (on rows) are compared in terms of feasibility, model coverage, TS size and TC length. Best values are in boldface. For them p-values are at the bottom.

	FEAS	COV	SZ	LEN
DFV	0.53	**0.74**	5.61	6.22
BFV	**0.64**	0.72	14.00	2.86
RAND	0.32	0.73	7.36	5.65
NGRAM2	**1.00**	**0.94**	5.61	6.98
NGRAM3	0.36	0.80	7.11	5.39
NGRAM4	0.36	0.78	7.22	5.64

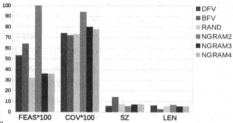

p-value(NGRAM2, BFV, FEAS) < 2.2e-16
p-value(NGRAM2, DFV, COV) = 1.475e-12

cases for Flexstore/Cyclos, each containing on average 3.38/2.86 events). The other methods are not very different from each other. DFV produced shorter test cases than NGRAM (and RAND) on Flexstore, while on Cyclos the difference is marginal. Overall, test suite size and test case length associated with NGRAM seem reasonable for the applications under test and in line with the values obtained from the other considered methods, with the exception of BFV, which produces many, very short test sequences.

5   Related Works

FSM models have been exploited to generate test cases in several existing works [13,15,16,19–22]. A survey on model based testing was conducted by Dias Neto et al. [1].

Test cases can be derived either from models specified at design time or from inferred models. In case of a design-time models, abstract test cases can be used to check how the expected behaviours (coming from the model) have been implemented in the application [19,20]. Hence, the role of behaviour specifications is to provide abstract test cases, test oracles, and a measure of the test adequacy [21].

Instead, the role of an inferred model is mainly to provide abstract test cases (e.g., [16,19,22]), to be instantiated in executable test cases by adding inputs and, eventually, test oracles (e.g., [16]). This instantiation is an expensive activity and the presence of infeasible test cases demand for substantial effort and knowledge from the tester's side, who is required to recognise them and filter them out. To the best of our knowledge, this is the first work which tries to address the problem of test case infeasibility by adopting a test case derivation strategy (based on the N-gram statistics) that aims at increasing the likelihood of feasibility and correspondingly the level of coverage actually achieved. While approaches exist which try to balance the degree of over/under approximation of inferred models [7] and metrics have been proposed to evaluate the generalisation capability of inferred models [23], this is the first work which tries to address the problem of test case infeasibility.

6   Conclusions and Future Work

In the context of model based testing, we have proposed a test sequence derivation strategy based on the N-gram statistics. To avoid (or limit) the generation of infeasible event sequences, the next event to add to a sequence is selected based on the frequency of occurrence of the N-tuple of events that ends with the event considered for addition. Experimental results show that the proposed approach generates a higher proportion of feasible test sequences than graph visit and random strategies. In turn, the higher proportion of feasible sequences increases the level of model coverage reached by the test suite.

In our future work we plan to extend the empirical study to additional subject applications. We intend to study empirically the role of the training material (i.e., the execution traces) used to learn the N-gram statistics, which is key for a successful application of the approach. We also plan to investigate the possibility of further increasing the coverage achieved by hybridising and extending the *N*-gram based method (e.g., through smoothing [9]).

Acknowledgments. This work has been funded by the European Union FP7 project FITTEST (grant agreement n. 257574).

References

1. Dias Neto, A.C., Subramanyan, R., Vieira, M., Travassos, G.H.: A survey on model-based testing approaches: a systematic review. In: Proceedings of the International Workshop on Empirical Assessment of Software Engineering Languages and Technologies (Co-located with ASE '07), WEASELTech '07, New York, USA, pp. 31–36. ACM (2007)
2. Mariani, L., Marchetto, A., Nguyen, C.D., Tonella, P., Baars, A.I.: Revolution: automatic evolution of mined specifications. In: Proceedings of the 23rd IEEE International Symposium on Software, Reliability Engineering (ISSRE), pp. 241–250 (2012)
3. Dallmeier, V., Lindig, C., Wasylkowski, A., Zeller, A.: Mining object behavior with ADABU. In: Proceedings of the 2006 International Workshop on Dynamic Systems Analysis WODA '06, New York, USA, pp. 17–24. ACM (2006)
4. Biermann, A., Feldman, J.: On the synthesis of finite-state machines from samples of their behavior. IEEE Trans. Comput. **21**(6), 592–597 (1972)
5. Krka, I., Brun, Y., Popescu, D., Garcia, J., Medvidovic, N.: Using dynamic execution traces and program invariants to enhance behavioral model inference. In: ICSE (2), pp. 179–182 (2010)
6. Lorenzoli, D., Mariani, L., Pezzè, M.: Automatic generation of software behavioral models. In: 30th International Conference on Software Engineering (ICSE). IEEE Computer Society (2008)
7. Tonella, P., Marchetto, A., Nguyen, C.D., Jia, Y., Lakhotia, K., Harman, M.: Finding the optimal balance between over and under approximation of models inferred from execution logs. In: Proceedings of the Fifth IEEE International Conference on Software Testing, Verification and Validation (ICST), pp. 21–30 (2012)
8. Hedley, D., Hennell, M.A.: The causes and effects of infeasible paths in computer programs. In: Proceedings of the 8th International Conference on Software Engineering ICSE '85, Los Alamitos, CA, USA, pp. 259–266. IEEE Computer Society Press (1985)
9. Jurafsky, D., Martin, J.H.: Speech and Language Processing: An Introduction to Speech Recognition, Computational Linguistics and Natural Language Processing. Pearson Prentice Hall, Englewood Cliffs (2007)
10. Pezzè, M., Young, M.: Software Testing and Analysis: Process Principles and Techniques. Wiley, Hoboken (2007)
11. Shafique, M., Labiche, Y.: A systematic review of model based testing tool support. Technical Report SCE-10-04, Carleton University, Canada (2010)
12. Briand, L.C., Labiche, Y.: A UML-based approach to system testing. In: Gogolla, M., Kobryn, C. (eds.) UML 2001. LNCS, vol. 2185, pp. 194–208. Springer, Heidelberg (2001)
13. Kim, Y., Hong, H., Bae, D., Cha, S.: Test cases generation from UML state diagrams. IEE Proc. Softw. **146**(4), 187–192 (1999)

14. Turner, C.D., Robson, D.J.: The state-based testing of object-oriented programs. In: Proceedings of the Conference on Software Maintenance (ICSM), Montreal, Canada, pp. 302–310. IEEE Computer Society (1993)

15. Yuan, X., Memon, A.M.: Using GUI run-time state as feedback to generate test cases. In: Proceedings the International Conference on Software Engineering (ICSE), Washington, DC, USA, pp. 396–405. IEEE Computer Society (2007)

16. Marchetto, A., Tonella, P., Ricca, F.: State-based testing of ajax web applications. In: Proceedings of IEEE International Conference on Software Testing (ICST), Lillehammer, Norway, pp. 121–131 (2008)

17. Andrews, A., Offutt, J., Alexander, R.: Testing web applications by modeling with FSMs. Softw. Syst. Model. 4(3), 326–345 (2005)

18. Dallmeier, V., Lindig, C., Wasylkowski, A., Zeller, A.: Mining object behavior with ADABU. In: Proceedings of the International Workshop on Dynamic Analysis (WODA), Shangai, China, pp. 17–24 (2006)

19. Dallmeier, V., Knopp, N., Mallon, C., Hack, S., Zeller, A.: Generating test cases for specification mining. In: Proceedings of the 19th International Symposium on Software Testing and Analysis ISSTA '10, New York, USA, pp. 85–96. ACM (2010)

20. Offutt, J., Abdurazik, A.: Generating tests from UML specifications. In: France, R., Rumpe, B. (eds.) UML 1999. LNCS, vol. 1723, pp. 416–429. Springer, Heidelberg (1999)

21. Stocks, P., Carrington, D.: A framework for specification-based testing. IEEE Trans. Softw. Eng. 22, 777–793 (1996)

22. Corbett, J.C., Dwyer, M.B., Hatcliff, J., Laubach, S., Pasareanu, C.S., Robby, Zheng, H.: Bandera: extracting finite-state models from java source code. In: Proceedings of the International Conference on Software Engineering, pp. 439–448 (2000)

23. Walkinshaw, N., Bogdanov, K., Damas, C., Lambeau, B., Dupont, P.: A framework for the competitive evaluation of model inference techniques. In: Proceedings of the International Workshop on Model Inference in Testing (MIIT) (2010)

Unit Testing Tool Competitions –
Lessons Learned

Sebastian Bauersfeld[1]([✉]), Tanja E.J. Vos[1], and Kiran Lakhotia[2]

[1] Centro de Métodos de Producción de Software (ProS),
Universidad Politécnica de Valencia, Valencia, Spain
{sbauersfeld,tvos}@pros.upv.es
http://www.pros.upv.es
[2] University College London, London, UK
k.lakhotia@cs.ucl.ac.uk
http://www.ucl.ac.uk/

Abstract. This paper reports about the two rounds of the Java Unit Testing Tool Competition that ran in the context of the Search Based Software Testing (SBST) workshop at ICST 2013 and the first Future Internet Testing (FITTEST) workshop at ICTSS 2013. It describes the main objectives of the benchmark, the Java classes that were selected in both competitions, the data that was collected, the tools that were used for data collection, the protocol that was carried out to execute the benchmark and how the final benchmark scores for each participating tool were calculated. Eventually, we discuss the challenges encountered during the events, what we learned and how we plan to improve our framework for future competitions.

Keywords: Benchmark · Mutation testing · Automated unit testing

1   Introduction

This paper describes the benchmark setup of the Java Unit Testing Tools competition. The goal of this competition is to have automated unit testing tools compete against each other. Each tool will be presented a previously selected set of Java classes for which it has to generate valid JUnit tests. The quality of these tests is then evaluated with measures such as achieved code and mutation coverage. We developed a benchmark score function which uses this data to compute a single number – the benchmark score – which is then used to create a ranking of all testing tools. Since the process of collecting this data is time-consuming and laborious, we developed an automated benchmark framework, which feeds the Classes Under Test (CUTs) to each competing tool, measures the quality of the resulting tests and yields the tool's final score. On the following pages we will describe the main aspects of this framework and the challenges encountered during the two rounds of the competition.

We directed the development of this benchmark after the work of Sim et al. [36], according to which a benchmark should have three parts: (1) a clearly

T.E.J. Vos, K. Lakhotia, and S. Bauersfeld (Eds.): FITTEST 2013, LNCS 8432, pp. 75–94, 2014.
DOI: 10.1007/978-3-319-07785-7_5, © Springer International Publishing Switzerland 2014

defined objective of what is and what can be evaluated (Sects. 2.1, 2.2, 3.1 and 3.2); (2) a task sample (Sects. 2.3, 2.7, 3.3 and 3.8); (3) and performance measures (Sects. 2.6, 2.8, 3.7 and 3.9). We will elaborate on each of these parts for both rounds of the competition.

2 First Round

The first round of the competition started in November 2012 and its results where presented during the Search Based Software Testing (SBST) workshop at ICST 2013. The following pages describe how we designed and carried out the competition.

2.1 Objective - What to Achieve?

The objective of the benchmark is to evaluate tools that generate JUnit test cases for Java classes. Evaluation will be done with respect to a benchmark score that takes into account test effectiveness (fault finding capability and coverage) and test efficiency (time to prepare, generate and execute the test cases). Prior to evaluation, the participating tools have no knowledge of the Java classes that constitute the benchmark, so the tools cannot be fine-tuned towards the specific artifacts under test. Two baselines for comparison will be used; each on an extreme end of the level of intelligence that is used for generating the test cases. On the one hand a random testing approach implemented by the tool Randoop [15]. On the other hand, the manually created tests that come with the classes that are part of the benchmark data.

2.2 Uniform Description of the Tools Being Studied

In order to be able to unify and combine the results of the benchmark and aggregate the results in secondary studies [20,27], we need to use a taxonomy (as [37] calls it) or a hierarchy (as [20] calls it) or a characterisation schema (as [38] calls it) of the tools under investigation. We decided to use the taxonomy from [37], that we have adapted to software testing and augmented with the results from [20,28,38].

To illustrate the resulting schema, Table 1 contains the description of baseline Randoop [30]. When the participants of the competition will publish their results, they will make use of this schema to describe their tools.

2.3 Selecting the Classes Under Test (CUTs)

The motivation for selecting the CUTs that constitute the benchmark was to have applications that are reasonably small, but not trivial, so that we can run the competition and finish it in restricted time. Therefore, we have selected classes from well-known test subjects used in the SBST community that come with a number of manually created JUnit test classes which we need for the

Table 1. Description of Randoop

Prerequisites	
Static or dynamic	Dynamic testing at the Java class level
Software type	Java classes
Lifecycle phase	Unit testing for Java programs
Environment	In principle all development environments, special versions/plugins exist for Eclipse and the Microsoft .NET platform
Knowledge required	JUnit unit testing for Java
Experience required	Basic unit testing knowledge
Input and output of the tool	
Input	Java classes (compiled)
Output	JUnit test cases (source)
Operation	
Interaction	Through the command line
User guidance	Through the command line
Source of information	Manuals and papers online [15]
Maturity	Mature research prototype (not under development anymore)
Technology behind the tool	Feedback-directed random testing
Obtaining the tool and information	
License	MIT license
Cost	Open source
Support	Developers need to be contacted directly
Empirical evidence about the tool	
Only studies about effectiveness have been found [21,30,31]	

previously stated baseline [19,22,29,35]. Classes, for which at least one manually written unit test existed in the project, were considered interesting, because developers had made the effort to write a unit test for them. We decided not to use the SF100 benchmark [23] because it is too large for the tools to complete in reasonable time for the competition and it contains many unconventional classes. Our final benchmark only contains some classes that are unconventional in that they contain difficult to test methods like for example a constructor that takes a file as an argument. These come from the sqlsheet [17] project.

Our competition relies on the coverage tool Cobertura [5] to collect coverage information and the mutation testing tool Javalanche [34] to compute the mutation score. Therefore, we further restricted the classes based on the limitations of each of those tools (and combined use).

2.4 Characteristics of the CUTs

Table 2 shows the characteristics of the classes that constitute the benchmark. *AMC* denotes the Average Method Complexity per Class, i.e. the sum of cyclomatic complexities of the methods of the given class divided by the amount of methods; LOC denotes the Lines of Code of the CUT; $TLOC$ denotes the Lines of Code of the corresponding manual JUnit test class; $TAss$ denotes the number of invocations of JUnit `assert<X>()` and `fail()` methods that occur in the code of the corresponding test class. These measures are given to aid benchmark participants in analyzing the strengths and weaknesses of their tools when comparing their results against the manual test cases.

2.5   Seeding Mutants

In order to be able to evaluate the fault finding effectiveness of the generated test cases, we decided to use the mutation testing tool Javalanche [34]. The purpose of mutation testing is to insert artificial faults into a program (i.e., faults a programmer might make), and assess how good test cases are at detecting those faults. In Javalanche a fault is considered detected (i.e., killed) if the result of running a unit test on the original program and the mutated version differs. This is typically indicated by a passing test failing on a mutant program and is akin to strong mutation testing [26]. Thus, the ability to kill mutants generated by Javalanche depends upon how thorough a test checks the output of a particular test execution. One example in which this can be done is by using JUnit `assert` functions to check properties of the class under test, or simply by checking the return value of a method under test (if applicable).

In theory one can generate a very large number of mutants, because a program typically has many statements or expressions that can be changed by a mutation tool. In order to make mutation testing tractable, Javalanche only implements a subset of all possible mutation operators. These are: replacing numerical constants, negating jump conditions, replacing arithmetic operators, and omitting method calls [34].

To further optimise the mutation testing process Javalanche uses mutant schemata. Instead of generating many copies of a class, each containing a single mutation, Javalanche adds all supported mutations for a particular class into a single instrumented class file. It uses guard statements to enable selective mutations and compute which mutants are detected by a test case. Furthermore, instead of executing *all* tests for each mutant, Javalanche uses coverage information of tests to determine a subset of tests to run for a particular mutant. In order for a test to kill a mutant it has to satisfy three requirements: (1) It must reach the mutated statement, (2) infect the program state after executing the mutant and (3) propagate the infected state to the output checked by the test oracle. Javalanche will only run those tests that can satisfy condition (1) for a particular mutation, since a test that does not exercise the piece of code containing the mutant, cannot kill that mutant.

2.6   Variables - Which Data to Collect?

Independent variables are the used testing tools $T_1 \ldots T_N$. Other factors which can impact the results are the selected CUTs from Table 2 and the mutants that

Table 2. The CUTs for the first round of the tool competition.

Number	Class	Project	AMC	LOC	TLOC	TAss	Reference
1	ArrayUtils	Apache Commons Lang	3.13	2046	2268	1025	[1]
2	Barcode	Barbecue	1.53	234	177	25	[4]
3	BaseDateTimeField	Joda Time	1.72	311	495	112	[13]
4	BlankModule	Barbecue	1.00	17	7	1	[4]
5	BooleanUtils	Apache Commons Lang	3.92	365	793	249	[1]
6	BuddhistChronology	Joda Time	1.63	99	301	164	[13]
7	CalendarConverter	Joda Time	2.20	54	121	28	[13]
8	CharRange	Apache Commons Lang	2.42	150	300	177	[1]
9	Chronology	Joda Time	1.00	116	230	72	[13]
10	CodabarBarcode	Barbecue	2.20	98	151	48	[4]
11	Code128Barcode	Barbecue	2.56	229	722	255	[4]
12	Code39Barcode	Barbecue	1.80	86	175	25	[4]
13	CompositeModule	Barbecue	1.42	49	59	5	[4]
14	ConverterManager	Joda Time	1.92	268	826	146	[13]
15	ConverterSet	Joda Time	5.33	178	144	19	[13]
16	DateConverter	Joda Time	1.00	17	74	17	[13]
17	DateTimeComparator	Joda Time	2.69	101	639	172	[13]
18	DateTimeFieldType	Joda Time	2.37	285	267	170	[13]
19	DateTimeFormat	Joda Time	4.02	437	824	176	[13]
20	DateTimeFormatter	Joda Time	1.88	284	545	178	[13]
21	DateTimeFormatterBuilder	Joda Time	2.89	1708	153	31	[13]
22	DateTimeUtils	Joda Time	1.86	156	322	57	[13]
23	DateTimeZone	Joda Time	2.41	518	723	207	[13]
24	Days	Joda Time	1.80	156	298	104	[13]
25	DefaultEnvironment	Barbecue	1.00	11	16	2	[4]
26	DurationField	Joda Time	1.09	34	31	5	[13]
27	DurationFieldType	Joda Time	2.29	150	140	67	[13]
28	EnvironmentFactory	Barbecue	1.50	45	48	6	[4]
29	FieldUtils	Joda Time	2.87	139	137	27	[13]
30	FixedBitSet	Apache Lucene	2.50	283	230	32	[2]
31	Fraction	Apache Commons Lang	3.73	443	1015	333	[1]
32	GJChronology	Joda Time	2.02	672	401	166	[13]
33	GraphicsOutput	Barbecue	1.83	51	73	13	[4]
34	GregorianChronology	Joda Time	1.82	121	224	135	[13]
35	HeadlessEnvironment	Barbecue	1.00	11	12	2	[4]
36	Hours	Joda Time	1.84	159	295	106	[13]
37	ISOChronology	Joda Time	1.53	110	359	174	[13]
38	ISODateTimeFormat	Joda Time	2.69	923	414	134	[13]
39	ISOPeriodFormat	Joda Time	1.83	116	132	41	[13]
40	IllegalFieldValueException	Joda Time	1.42	167	291	160	[13]
41	Int2of5Barcode	Barbecue	1.50	39	75	9	[4]
42	LenientChronology	Joda Time	1.88	84	111	19	[13]
43	LinearBarcode	Barbecue	2.33	41	161	16	[4]
44	LongConverter	Joda Time	1.00	18	73	18	[13]
45	MillisDurationField	Joda Time	1.09	81	156	48	[13]
46	Minutes	Joda Time	1.65	144	280	96	[13]
47	Module	Barbecue	2.00	64	67	15	[4]
48	ModuleFactory	Barbecue	1.75	383	33	9	[4]
49	Modulo10	Barbecue	1.75	29	30	7	[4]
50	Months	Joda Time	2.29	151	250	99	[13]
51	MutableDateTime	Joda Time	1.22	454	178	26	[13]
52	NullConverter	Joda Time	1.00	27	133	27	[13]
53	NumberUtils	Apache Commons Lang	5.00	636	1049	507	[1]
54	OffsetDateTimeField	Joda Time	1.19	90	431	119	[13]
55	PeriodFormat	Joda Time	1.50	38	82	6	[13]
56	PeriodFormatter	Joda Time	1.47	117	171	34	[13]
57	PeriodFormatterBuilder	Joda Time	3.46	1166	679	308	[13]
58	PeriodType	Joda Time	2.30	472	757	450	[13]
59	PreciseDateTimeField	Joda Time	1.42	47	541	119	[13]
60	PreciseDurationDateTimeField	Joda Time	1.50	62	541	123	[13]
61	PreciseDurationField	Joda Time	1.27	52	208	66	[13]
62	ReadableDurationConverter	Joda Time	1.25	27	77	20	[13]
63	ReadableInstantConverter	Joda Time	1.80	40	97	28	[13]
64	ReadableIntervalConverter	Joda Time	1.50	41	137	41	[13]
65	ReadablePartialConverter	Joda Time	1.39	35	101	17	[13]
66	ReadablePeriodConverter	Joda Time	1.00	22	72	20	[13]
67	ScaledDurationField	Joda Time	1.29	80	224	67	[13]
68	Seconds	Joda Time	1.65	144	272	93	[13]
69	SeparatorModule	Barbecue	1.00	19	10	2	[4]
70	Std2of5Barcode	Barbecue	1.62	58	77	9	[4]
71	StringConverter	Joda Time	5.71	133	460	168	[13]
72	UCCEAN128Barcode	Barbecue	5.11	180	54	8	[4]
73	UnsupportedDateTimeField	Joda Time	1.11	195	374	104	[13]
74	WeakIdentityMap	Apache Lucene	1.55	130	200	53	[2]
75	XlsSheetIterator	sqlsheet	8.50	235	60	20	[17]
76	XlsxSheetIterator	sqlsheet	6.20	256	55	18	[17]
77	Years	Joda Time	1.85	124	232	81	[13]

have been seeded by Javalanche. Dependent variables are effectiveness (coverage) and efficiency (time). The following measures are used to calculate the benchmark-score for each T_i $(1 \leq i \leq N)$:

t_{prep} preparation time that T_i needs before it starts generating test cases (i.e. instrumentation, etc.)

And for each class listed in Table 2:

t_{gen} time it takes to generate the test cases
t_{exec} time it takes to execute these test cases
cov_l line coverage (measured by Cobertura [5])
cov_b branch coverage (measured by Cobertura [5])
cov_m mutation coverage (measured by Javalanche [34]).

2.7 Protocol - How has the Benchmark been Carried Out?

Figure 1 shows the architecture of the framework used to carry out the competition. T_1 to T_N are the testing tools that participated in the competition. Each

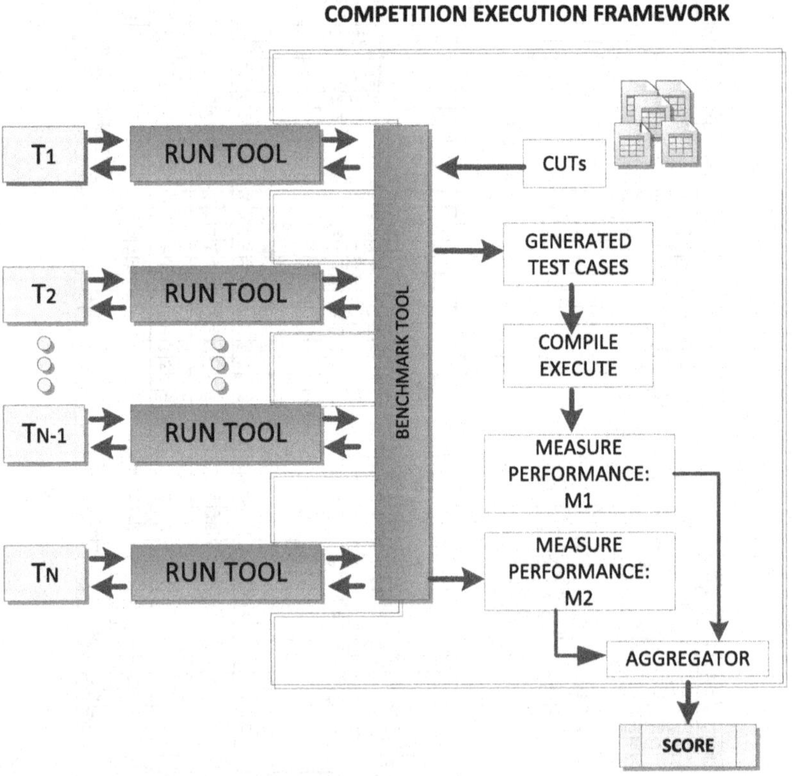

Fig. 1. Competition execution framework

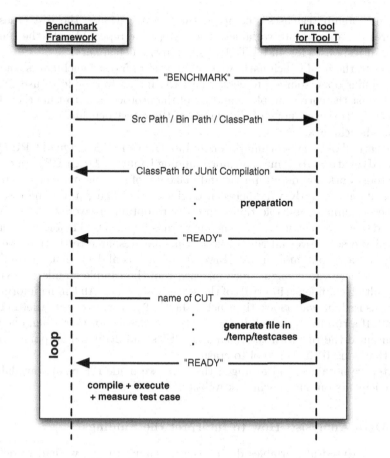

Fig. 2. Benchmark automation protocol

participant had to implement a *run tool*, which is a wrapper around the actual testing tool T_i and enables communication with the benchmark framework. It implements a simple protocol over the standard input and output streams, as depicted in Fig. 2. The benchmark framework starts the protocol by sending the string "BENCHMARK" to the standard output stream. It proceeds by sending the location of the SUT's source code, the compiled class files and its dependencies (the Java classpath). Once the run tool received this information, it may inform the framework about its own dependencies which might be necessary to compile the generated unit test cases. It therefore can send a classpath string to the framework to be used during the compilation stage. Once it has done this, it will emit "READY" to inform the framework that it awaits the testing challenges. The Framework then starts to send the fully qualified name of the first CUT to stdout. The run tool reads this name, analyzes the class, generates a unit test and creates one or more JUnit test case files in the "temp/testcases" directory. Then, it emits "READY", after which the framework looks into "temp/testcases", compiles the file(s), executes the test cases and measures the appropriate variables. These steps are repeated until the run tool generated responses for all CUT challenges in the benchmark.

Prior to the final benchmark, we offered a set of 5 test benchmarks compiled from popular open source projects. The participants were able to use these in order to test the correct implementation of the protocol and to tune their tool's parameters. However, none of the classes of these test benchmarks were part of the final benchmark.

We carried out the benchmarks on an Intel(R) Core(TM)2 Quad CPU Q9550 @ 2.83 GHz with 8 GB of main memory running Ubuntu 12.04. 1 LTS. Since most of the tools work non-deterministic and make use of random number generation, the results can slightly vary between distinct runs. Thus, it was necessary to run the benchmark multiple times, in order to obtain an average value for the achieved score. We carried out 6 benchmark runs for each tool before we averaged the achieved score over all runs. Due to time and resource restrictions we were unable to carry out more runs. However, we are confident that the obtained results are accurate enough, since for each tool the sample standard deviation and resulting confidence intervals of the scores were small. All timing information was measured in wall clock time using Java's `System.currentTimeMillis()` method. If a run tool crashed during a run or got stuck for more than one hour, we continued the run with the remaining CUTs and deducted all points for the CUT that caused the run tool to crash.

After we obtained and averaged the data, we made the results available to all participants on our benchmark website.

2.8   Data Analysis - How to Interpret the Findings?

Having measured all variables during the benchmark runs, we had to define a ranking scheme in order to determine which tool performed best. We defined the two most important indicators of a tool's quality to be the time needed to pass the benchmark and the ability of the generated tests to kill mutants. In addition, we rewarded a tool's ability to generate tests with good code coverage. To express the quality of a tool T as a single number, we defined a benchmark function which assigns to each run of a test tool T a score as a weighted sum over the measured variables:

$$score_T := \sum_{class} \left[\omega_l \cdot cov_l(class) + \omega_b \cdot cov_b(class) + \right.$$
$$\left. \omega_m \cdot cov_m(class) \right] -$$
$$\omega_t \cdot \left(t_{prep} + \sum_{class} \left[t_{gen}(class) + t_{exec}(class) \right] \right)$$

where, consistent with Sect. 2.6, cov_l, cov_b, cov_m refer to achieved line, branch and mutation coverage and t_{prep}, t_{gen}, t_{exec} refer to the tool's preparation time, test case generation time and test case execution time, measured in hours. ω_l, ω_b, ω_m and ω_t are the weights, for which we chose the values $\omega_l = 1$, $\omega_b = 2$, $\omega_m = 4$ and $\omega_t = 5$. As mentioned before, we chose time and the ability to kill mutants to be the most important quality indicators, thus ω_t and ω_m have been assigned the highest values. Since it is generally more difficult to obtain a good branch coverage than a good line coverage, we chose ω_b to be two times the value of ω_l. The reason why we included line coverage, is to compensate for Cobertura's non-standard definition of branch coverage, where methods without conditional statements are considered branch-free. Therefore, in the worst case, it is possible to obtain 100 % branch coverage, but at the same time achieving only extremely low line coverage.

In order to obtain a benchmark score for the manual test cases, it would be necessary to obtain the value of t_{gen} for each class. Since we do not know how much time the developers of the manual tests spent writing the corresponding JUnit classes, we cannot directly calculate a score for the manual case.

The benchmark function and the chosen weight values have been announced several days before the start of the benchmark, so that the participants were able to tune their tools' parameters.

2.9 Benchmark Results for the Baselines

Table 3 shows the benchmark results for Randoop and manual testing, averaged over 6 runs. Since we only have 6 samples, we calculated the confidence interval for the Randoop score using Student's t-distribution and Bessel's Correction to estimate the standard deviation from the sample data. For manual testing we cannot assign a concrete benchmark score, since we do not know the values for t_{gen}. Instead, we provide the score as a function of t_{gen}.

For convenience during interpretation, we listed t_{gen}, t_{exec} and t_{prep} in seconds. However, for the calculation of the benchmark score, the measures are converted to hours.

Information about the results achieved by the participants' tools and their interpretations can be found in [24, 32].

3   Second Round

The following pages describe the benchmark setup of the second Java Unit Testing Tool Competition that ran during the Future Internet Testing (FITTEST) workshop at ICTSS 2013. Again, the goal is to compare the performance of automated unit testing tools against each other and against manually generated unit tests. However, this time we put more emphasis on finding out whether automated tools are ready to replace certain tasks of human testers. After talking to the participants and discussing the positive and negative aspects of the benchmark framework, we changed the following aspects of the competition:

1. We reduced the impact of generation time in the final benchmark score. The reason for this is, that we think that it is more important that a tool generates

Table 3. Final results for the first round of the tool competition: on the left: Randoop. On the right: manual testing. More information about the participants' tools in [24,32].

Results for Randoop

Class — values averaged over 6 runs, times in seconds — t_{prep} = 0.1525 seconds

Class	t_{gen} (s)	t_{exec} (s)	cov_l	cov_b	cov_m
1	101.34	0.08	0.8538	0.6954	0.0312
2	100.35	0.00	0.0000	0.0000	0.0000
3	100.38	0.00	1.0000	0.0000	0.0000
4	102.13	0.16	0.4286	1.0000	0.4333
5	101.50	0.10	0.7211	0.5547	0.0344
6	101.20	0.00	0.0000	0.0000	0.0000
7	100.31	0.00	0.0000	0.0000	0.0000
8	100.32	0.00	0.0000	0.0000	0.0000
9	100.38	0.00	1.0000	0.0000	0.0000
10	100.58	0.08	0.5179	0.2083	0.0207
11	102.07	0.54	0.7714	0.4457	0.0077
12	101.87	0.46	1.0000	1.0000	0.0000
13	101.45	0.04	0.6800	0.6667	0.3394
14	102.52	4.12	0.5349	0.3548	0.0000
15	100.33	0.00	0.0000	0.0000	0.0000
16	100.33	0.00	0.0000	1.0000	0.0000
17	100.98	0.73	0.6786	0.5435	0.0030
18	100.30	0.00	0.0000	1.0000	0.0000
19	100.47	0.03	0.3300	0.1469	0.0449
20	100.39	0.00	0.0000	0.0000	0.0000
21	100.95	0.04	0.7981	0.6003	0.0226
22	100.35	0.01	0.2432	0.0789	0.0000
23	100.36	0.00	0.0000	0.0000	0.0000
24	100.98	0.10	0.6494	0.4103	0.0053
25	101.97	0.03	1.0000	1.0000	1.0000
26	100.31	0.00	0.0000	0.0000	0.0000
27	100.31	0.00	0.0000	1.0000	0.0000
28	100.30	0.00	0.7037	0.5000	0.0000
29	114.73	0.00	0.0000	0.0000	0.0000
30	101.23	1.53	0.9688	0.5325	0.0000
31	100.91	0.00	0.0000	0.0000	0.0000
32	101.13	0.11	0.8480	0.7273	0.0174
33	100.36	0.00	0.0000	0.0000	0.0000
34	101.14	0.07	0.7627	0.5714	0.0093
35	105.40	0.07	1.0000	1.0000	1.0000
36	101.12	0.12	0.6456	0.4000	0.0056
37	101.35	0.07	0.9111	0.7500	0.0181
38	100.40	0.07	0.7340	0.3511	0.0020
39	100.36	0.02	0.9783	0.5000	0.0000
40	104.38	0.67	0.4561	0.5000	0.4883
41	100.47	0.02	0.2667	0.5000	0.1765
42	101.19	0.00	0.0000	0.0000	0.0000
43	100.39	0.00	0.0000	0.0000	0.0000
44	100.36	0.00	0.0000	1.0000	0.0000
45	100.39	0.00	0.0000	0.0000	0.0000
46	101.33	0.13	0.6667	0.4571	0.0047
47	101.14	0.05	0.6571	0.6111	0.4340
48	100.42	0.01	0.9887	0.7000	0.0007
49	100.36	0.00	0.8000	0.6250	0.3696
50	100.98	0.08	0.6582	0.4773	0.0048
51	101.28	1.09	0.7081	0.1622	0.0000
52	100.39	0.00	0.0000	1.0000	0.0000
53	104.08	0.15	0.6756	0.4594	0.0900
54	102.31	0.00	0.0000	0.0000	0.0000
55	100.35	0.01	0.9333	0.5000	0.0000
56	100.46	0.00	0.0000	0.0000	0.0000
57	101.11	0.05	0.9180	0.6835	0.0478
58	100.95	0.03	0.8430	0.6731	0.0587
59	100.36	0.00	0.0000	0.0000	0.0000
60	100.33	0.00	0.0000	0.0000	0.0000
61	100.35	0.00	0.0000	0.0000	0.0000
62	100.38	0.00	0.0000	0.0000	0.0000
63	100.41	0.00	0.0000	0.0000	0.0000
64	100.40	0.00	0.0000	0.0000	0.0000
65	100.39	0.00	0.0000	0.0000	0.0000
66	100.40	0.00	0.0000	1.0000	0.0000
67	100.73	0.00	0.0000	0.0000	0.0000
68	100.98	0.06	0.6667	0.4571	0.0047
69	101.68	0.04	0.6250	1.0000	0.4638
70	102.00	0.34	1.0000	0.9000	0.0000
71	100.38	0.00	0.0000	0.0000	0.0000
72	101.86	0.54	0.6992	0.5789	0.0000
73	100.39	0.00	0.0000	0.0000	0.0000
74	101.28	0.06	0.9677	0.8333	0.2162
75	100.42	0.00	0.0000	0.0000	0.0000
76	100.40	0.00	0.0000	0.0000	0.0000
77	101.21	0.06	0.6393	0.4857	0.0048
Score	**101.8129** (CI = [100.10, 103.52] with α = 0.05)				

Results Manual

Class — values averaged over 6 runs, times in seconds — t_{prep} = 0.00 seconds

Class	t_{gen} (s)	t_{exec} (s)	cov_l	cov_b	cov_m
1	unknown	0.08	0.6567	0.7830	0.0170
2	unknown	0.49	0.6991	0.6176	0.1218
3	unknown	0.08	0.7515	0.6111	0.0753
4	unknown	0.00	0.4286	1.0000	0.0500
5	unknown	0.01	1.0000	0.9609	0.0337
6	unknown	0.01	0.9259	0.7857	0.0121
7	unknown	0.06	1.0000	1.0000	0.6129
8	unknown	0.03	1.0000	0.9200	0.4346
9	unknown	0.14	1.0000	1.0000	0.0038
10	unknown	0.01	0.9643	0.9167	0.0925
11	unknown	0.12	0.9857	0.8913	0.0052
12	unknown	0.01	1.0000	1.0000	0.0238
13	unknown	0.01	0.7200	0.6667	0.1368
14	unknown	0.06	1.0000	1.0000	0.1226
15	unknown	0.01	0.7222	0.6938	0.4240
16	unknown	0.01	1.0000	1.0000	0.7059
17	unknown	0.07	0.9821	0.8696	0.0041
18	unknown	0.05	0.9867	1.0000	0.0075
19	unknown	0.10	0.7550	0.6573	0.0171
20	unknown	0.03	0.9294	0.7647	0.0205
21	unknown	0.06	0.6243	0.5825	0.0209
22	unknown	0.09	0.9459	1.0000	0.0040
23	unknown	0.14	0.8966	0.8188	0.0088
24	unknown	0.07	1.0000	0.9744	0.0045
25	unknown	0.00	1.0000	1.0000	0.1429
26	unknown	0.04	1.0000	1.0000	0.0028
27	unknown	0.04	0.9667	1.0000	0.0025
28	unknown	0.00	0.7407	0.7500	0.6364
29	unknown	0.00	0.1899	0.2069	0.2500
30	unknown	0.84	0.7604	0.3766	0.0584
31	unknown	0.11	0.9774	0.9184	0.1608
32	unknown	0.09	0.9006	0.8182	0.0205
33	unknown	0.01	0.5667	0.4000	0.1860
34	unknown	0.03	0.8475	0.6071	0.0183
35	unknown	0.00	1.0000	1.0000	0.3448
36	unknown	0.06	1.0000	0.9750	0.0040
37	unknown	0.07	0.9333	0.8125	0.0222
38	unknown	0.04	0.5455	0.3664	0.0213
39	unknown	0.01	1.0000	1.0000	0.0341
40	unknown	0.07	0.9474	0.7500	0.0035
41	unknown	0.01	0.8667	0.8333	0.0811
42	unknown	0.04	0.6863	0.3125	0.0165
43	unknown	0.02	1.0000	0.7500	0.2903
44	unknown	0.01	1.0000	1.0000	0.7222
45	unknown	0.03	1.0000	1.0000	0.0394
46	unknown	0.05	1.0000	0.9714	0.0036
47	unknown	0.01	0.7714	0.8333	0.2044
48	unknown	0.01	0.9887	0.7000	0.0006
49	unknown	0.00	0.8667	1.0000	0.8261
50	unknown	0.05	1.0000	0.9773	0.0049
51	unknown	0.06	0.2228	0.2162	0.0059
52	unknown	0.02	1.0000	1.0000	0.7727
53	unknown	0.01	0.9786	0.8712	0.1309
54	unknown	0.04	0.9487	0.7500	0.0681
55	unknown	0.02	1.0000	1.0000	0.0352
56	unknown	0.02	1.0000	0.8636	0.0335
57	unknown	0.02	0.8962	0.7848	0.0472
58	unknown	0.06	0.9522	0.8750	0.0074
59	unknown	0.04	0.9524	0.8333	0.0744
60	unknown	0.04	0.9630	0.9000	0.0771
61	unknown	0.04	1.0000	1.0000	0.0672
62	unknown	0.00	0.4167	0.0000	0.3750
63	unknown	0.01	1.0000	1.0000	0.6786
64	unknown	0.02	1.0000	1.0000	0.6970
65	unknown	0.02	1.0000	1.0000	0.6429
66	unknown	0.01	1.0000	1.0000	0.5000
67	unknown	0.04	1.0000	0.9286	0.0717
68	unknown	0.06	1.0000	0.9714	0.0042
69	unknown	0.00	1.0000	1.0000	0.1549
70	unknown	0.01	0.8889	0.8000	0.0902
71	unknown	0.04	0.9551	0.9242	0.1065
72	unknown	0.02	0.2602	0.1842	0.2231
73	unknown	0.03	0.9710	0.9167	0.0627
74	unknown	1.98	1.0000	0.8333	0.8304
75	unknown	12.33	0.5203	0.6479	0.2715
76	unknown	18.14	0.8043	0.7037	0.3214
77	unknown	0.05	1.0000	0.9714	0.0054
Score Function	$246.56 - 5 \cdot \sum_{class} t_{gen}(class)$ (t_{gen} in h))				

good tests, than how much time it needs for the generation. Of course, it should not use excessive time to generate results, but since the generation is fully automatic, time should be less of a factor than the ability to reveal faults. Thus we reduced the weight for test generation in the score formula, as described in Sect. 2.8

2. We instructed our own testers to write unit tests and measured the time it took them to finish the tests. During the last competition we only used the tests that came with the CUTs of the open source projects. We did not know the time it took the original testers to write these tests and were thus unable to assign a benchmark score to the manual testing approach. In this competition we can directly compare the manual and automated approaches to each other.

3. We exchanged the components used to measure code and mutation coverage. During the last benchmark we used Javalanche [34] and Cobertura [5]. Unfortunately, these tools are not maintained anymore and do not properly support Java 7, which caused problems with some of the participants' applications, which required to run on modern Java virtual machines. For this competition we integrated JaCoCo [10] and PITest [14] for code and mutation coverage.

In the following sections we will describe our benchmark setup, the measured variables, the score formula and present the results of the competition.

3.1   Objective - What to Achieve?

As in the first round of the competition, the objective of the benchmark is to evaluate tools that generate JUnit test cases for Java classes. Evaluation will be done with respect to a benchmark score that takes into account test effectiveness (fault finding capability and coverage) and test efficiency (time to prepare, generate and execute the test cases). Again, we will have two baselines for comparison: Randoop [15] on the one hand and manually created tests on the other hand. However, in this edition of the benchmark, we specifically ordered three different testers to write these tests, so that we would be able to measure the time they need.

3.2   Uniform Description of the Tools Being Studied

We will use the same schema that we applied in the first round. The descriptions of the competitors' tools can be found in [25, 33].

3.3   Selecting the CUTs

Our main motivation for CUT selection was to find out how the competing testing tools perform on popular open-source projects. Therefore, we have selected classes from the three well-known open source repositories Google Code[1], Sourceforge[2] and GitHub[3]. We narrowed our search to Java libraries, because we believe that these contain high-quality, difficult to test code. Altogether, our benchmark constitutes 63 classes selected from 9 projects.

---

[1] https://code.google.com/
[2] http://sourceforge.net/
[3] https://github.com/

To select the projects and the CUTs we used the following procedure:

1. We selected 3 projects per repository, i.e. 3 Google Code projects, 3 Source-forge projects and 3 GitHub projects.
2. We selected 7 classes per project.
3. For each repository we applied the search term "Java library" which resulted in a list of projects, ranked according to popularity.
4. We selected the three most popular projects from each repository. However, since the evaluated unit testing tools are designed for desktop operating systems, we only considered classic Java projects and ignored software written for Android devices,
5. From each of the projects, we selected the package with the highest value for the *Afferent Coupling Metric*. The AFC determines the number of classes from other packages that depend on classes in the current package. The reason why we decided to do so was to set the focus on "popular" classes within a project.
6. From each package, we selected classes with the highest maximal *Nested Block Depth*. The NBD determines the maximal depth of nested statements such as if-else constructs, loops and exception handlers. The motivation was to select complex classes for which it is difficult to achieve high branch coverage.

3.4   Characteristics of the CUTs

Table 4 shows the characteristics of the classes that constitute the benchmark. *LOC* denotes the Lines of Code of the CUT. *Max NBD* denotes the maximal Nested Block Depth and *Abstract* signals whether the CUT is abstract (which might be important for the interpretation of the results since some tools are not able to create test cases for abstract classes).

3.5   Seeding Mutants

In order to be able to evaluate the fault finding effectiveness of the generated test cases, we used the mutation testing tool PITest [14]. We decided to replace Javalanche [34], which we used in the previous competition, but which was not maintained anymore and did not work with byte code generated by the Java 7 compiler.

The set of mutation operators implemented by PITest are: Conditional boundary mutation (CB), negate conditional mutation (NC), math mutation (M), increment mutation (I), invert negatives mutation (IN), return value mutation (RV) and void method call mutation (VMC) [14].

3.6   The Baselines

As in the previous competition, in order to be able to compare the competing tools with reasonable baselines, we also ran the benchmark with

Table 4. The CUTs for the second round of the tool competition.

Number	Class	Project	LOC	max NBD	Abstract	Source	Reference
1	SearchException	Hibernate	15	1		Sourceforge.net	[9]
2	Version	Hibernate	12	1		Sourceforge.net	[9]
3	BackendFactory	Hibernate	72	2		Sourceforge.net	[9]
4	FlushLuceneWork	Hibernate	26	2		Sourceforge.net	[9]
5	OptimizeLuceneWork	Hibernate	26	2		Sourceforge.net	[9]
6	LoggerFactory	Hibernate	14	1		Sourceforge.net	[9]
7	LoggerHelper	Hibernate	17	1		Sourceforge.net	[9]
8	OAuthConfig	Scribe	63	3		GitHub	[16]
9	OAuthRequest	Scribe	36	2		GitHub	[16]
10	ParameterList	Scribe	95	3		GitHub	[16]
11	Request	Scribe	213	2		GitHub	[16]
12	Response	Scribe	72	2		GitHub	[16]
13	Token	Scribe	64	2		GitHub	[16]
14	Verifier	Scribe	15	1		GitHub	[16]
15	ExceptionDiagnosis	Twitter4j	73	4		GitHub	[18]
16	GeoQuery	Twitter4j	126	2		GitHub	[18]
17	OEmbedRequest	Twitter4j	147	2		GitHub	[18]
18	Paging	Twitter4j	171	3		GitHub	[18]
19	TwitterBaseImpl	Twitter4j	328	5	X	GitHub	[18]
20	TwitterException	Twitter4j	237	4		GitHub	[18]
21	TwitterImpl	Twitter4j	1187	3		GitHub	[18]
22	AsyncHttpClient	Async Http Client	296	5		GitHub	[3]
23	AsyncHttpClientConfig	Async Http Client	621	2		GitHub	[3]
24	FluentCaseInsensitiveStringsMap	Async Http Client	292	4		GitHub	[3]
25	FluentStringsMap	Async Http Client	240	4		GitHub	[3]
26	Realm	Async Http Client	481	3		GitHub	[3]
27	RequestBuilderBase	Async Http Client	544	6	X	GitHub	[3]
28	SimpleAsyncHttpClient	Async Http Client	610	3		GitHub	[3]
29	AttributeHelper	GData Java Client	344	4		Google Code	[7]
30	DateTime	GData Java Client	264	5		Google Code	[7]
31	Kind	GData Java Client	189	5		Google Code	[7]
32	Link	GData Java Client	190	4		Google Code	[7]
33	OtherContent	GData Java Client	179	4		Google Code	[7]
34	OutOfLineContent	GData Java Client	102	4		Google Code	[7]
35	Source	GData Java Client	324	4		Google Code	[7]
36	CharMatcher	Guava	824	4	X	Google Code	[8]
37	Joiner	Guava	222	3		Google Code	[8]
38	Objects	Guava	130	4		Google Code	[8]
39	Predicates	Guava	379	3		Google Code	[8]
40	SmallCharMatcher	Guava	92	4		Google Code	[8]
41	Splitter	Guava	266	4		Google Code	[8]
42	Suppliers	Guava	172	4		Google Code	[8]
43	CategoryDescendantsIterator	JWPL	103	4		Google Code	[12]
44	CycleHandler	JWPL	71	4		Google Code	[12]
45	Page	JWPL	351	4		Google Code	[12]
46	PageIterator	JWPL	182	7		Google Code	[12]
47	PageQueryIterable	JWPL	131	3		Google Code	[12]
48	Title	JWPL	79	2		Google Code	[12]
49	WikipediaInfo	JWPL	222	6		Google Code	[12]
50	AbstractLoader	eclipse-cs	77	3	X	Sourceforge.net	[6]
51	AnnotationUtility	eclipse-cs	78	4		Sourceforge.net	[6]
52	AutomaticBean	eclipse-cs	178	4		Sourceforge.net	[6]
53	FileContents	eclipse-cs	161	4		Sourceforge.net	[6]
54	FileText	eclipse-cs	184	4		Sourceforge.net	[6]
55	ScopeUtils	eclipse-cs	189	4		Sourceforge.net	[6]
56	Utils	eclipse-cs	160	4		Sourceforge.net	[6]
57	AbstractInstance	JMLL	136	2	X	Sourceforge.net	[11]
58	Complex	JMLL	53	1		Sourceforge.net	[11]
59	DefaultDataset	JMLL	152	3		Sourceforge.net	[11]
60	DenseInstance	JMLL	155	3		Sourceforge.net	[11]
61	Fold	JMLL	201	2		Sourceforge.net	[11]
62	SparseInstance	JMLL	191	3		Sourceforge.net	[11]
63	ARFFHandler	JMLL	51	6		Sourceforge.net	[11]

1. Randoop [15], a popular random test tool which is able to output JUnit test cases. We measured the results for Randoop the same way as we did with the competing unit testing tools.
2. Manually generated JUnit tests for the classes under test.

However, this time, instead of using the test cases shipped with the open-source projects, we instructed three testers with different profiles to write manual test cases for the CUTs. The first tester has several years of experience in industry and is currently employed in a testing company. The second one is a researcher working on search-based testing techniques and the third one a student. Each of them wrote test cases for 21 of the CUTs and recorded the time it took to get familiar with each class and to write the actual test case. Each tester decided on his own how much time he would spend on writing the tests and when to stop. None of the mentioned testers is also the author of one of the CUTs.

3.7   Variables - Which Data to Collect?

Independent variables are the used testing tools $T_1 \ldots T_N$. Other factors which can impact the results are the selected CUTs from Table 4 and the mutants that have been seeded by PITest. Dependent variables are effectiveness (coverage) and efficiency (time). This time, the competition relies on the coverage tool JaCoCo [10] to collect coverage information. The following measures are used to calculate the benchmark-score for each T_i ($1 \leq i \leq N$):

t_{prep} preparation time that T_i needs before it starts generating test cases (i.e. instrumentation, etc.)

And for each class listed in Table 4:

t_{gen} time it takes to generate the test cases
t_{exec} time it takes to execute these test cases
cov_i instruction coverage (measured by JaCoCo [10])
cov_b branch coverage (measured by JaCoCo)
cov_m mutation coverage (measured by PITest [14]).

3.8   Protocol - How has the Benchmark been Carried Out?

We used the same protocol (Fig. 2), framework architecture (Fig. 1) and hardware as in the first round of the competition. Although the benchmark framework had the same interface, we improved certain aspects of the implementation. In particular using JaCoCo and PITest made the test runs much faster and more reliable. We also switched to the Java 7 compiler and runtime environment, since some of the competitors' tools required new language features.

To prepare the settings for their tools, the competitors were allowed to use the CUTs from the previous benchmark.

3.9   Data Analysis - How to Interpret the Findings?

We interpreted the results the same way as we did in the first competition, using the benchmark formula described in Sect. 2.8. However, based on the experience from the last round, we adjusted the value of the weight factor for the generation time to be $\omega_t = 1$ instead of $\omega_t = 5$. As previously mentioned, the intend was to reduce the impact of generation time on the final benchmark score. After a discussion with the participants, we came to the conclusion that it is more important that a tool generates good tests, than how much time it needs for their generation. Thus, the ability to kill mutants was chosen to be the most important quality indicator, and consequently ω_m has been assigned the highest value.

3.10   Benchmark Results

Table 5 shows the benchmark results for each tool and the baselines averaged over 7 runs. For convenience during interpretation, we listed t_{gen}, t_{exec} and t_{prep} in minutes. However, for the calculation of the benchmark score, the values are converted to hours.

4   Threats to Validity of the Studies Performed

Conclusion Validity. The following threats could affect the ability to draw the correct conclusion about relations between our treatments (testing tools) and their respective outcomes:

1. Reliability of Treatment Implementation: This means that there is a risk that application of treatments to subjects is not similar. In order to reduce this threat, a clear protocol was designed, by giving the same instructions to all participants (developers of testing tools that will be evaluated) of the unit testing tool competition.
2. Reliability of Measures: Unreliable measures can invalidate our competition. We tried to be as objective as possible for measuring the test efficiency and effectiveness. For example, all timing information was measured in wall clock time using Java's System.currentTimeMillis () method. Effectiveness measures were automatically measured by Cobertura [5] and Javalanche [34] or JaCoCo [10] and PITest [14], respectively. Each of these tools is widely used in the testing community but could still contain faults that might threaten the validity of the results. Furthermore, Cobertura and JaCoCo have a non-standard definition of branch coverage, where methods without conditional statements are considered branch-free and hence result in a 100 % branch coverage. To compensate for this, we also included instruction coverage in the benchmark score. Finally, as the participants' tools are based on non-deterministic algorithms, it was necessary to run the benchmark multiple

Table 5. Final results for the second round of the tool competition

Variable (values averaged over 7 runs, times in minutes (if not otherwise specified), coverage is in percent)

Class	Manual $t_{prep}=0.00$					Randoop $t_{prep}=0.00$					EvoSuite $t_{prep}=0.00$					T3 $t_{prep}=0.00$				
	t_{gen}	t_{exec}	cov_i	cov_b	cov_m	t_{gen}	t_{exec}	cov_i	cov_b	cov_m	t_{gen}	t_{exec}	cov_i	cov_b	cov_m	t_{gen}	t_{exec}	cov_i	cov_b	cov_m
1	2.58	0.01	100.00	0.00	0.00	1.68	0.02	100.00	0.00	0.00	3.23	0.00	0.00	0.00	0.00	0.24	0.66	100.00	0.00	0.00
2	2.00	0.01	100.00	0.00	100.00	1.67	0.01	100.00	0.00	0.00	3.74	0.01	60.00	0.00	0.00	0.03	0.16	70.00	0.00	0.00
3	52.12	0.01	100.00	93.75	93.33	1.67	0.01	2.26	0.00	0.00	4.53	0.02	27.71	6.25	40.95	0.09	0.11	27.82	6.25	33.33
4	10.93	0.01	100.00	100.00	100.00	1.67	0.00	0.00	0.00	0.00	3.22	0.03	89.74	100.00	75.00	0.12	0.53	61.54	50.00	50.00
5	5.33	0.01	100.00	100.00	100.00	1.67	0.00	0.00	0.00	0.00	3.22	0.03	89.74	100.00	75.00	0.13	0.53	61.54	50.00	50.00
6	5.20	0.01	90.63	0.00	100.00	1.67	0.01	56.25	0.00	50.00	7.75	0.01	17.41	0.00	0.00	0.09	0.06	46.88	0.00	50.00
7	5.27	0.01	100.00	0.00	33.33	1.67	0.01	70.83	0.00	33.33	3.73	0.01	87.50	0.00	33.33	0.16	0.16	58.33	0.00	33.33
8	15.00	0.01	91.14	100.00	100.00	1.71	0.19	68.35	50.00	88.89	3.21	0.05	91.14	100.00	100.00	0.04	0.30	70.89	75.00	88.89
9	20.00	0.01	100.00	100.00	80.00	1.67	0.00	0.00	0.00	0.00	3.15	0.03	100.00	100.00	80.00	0.21	0.72	44.44	0.00	40.00
10	30.00	0.01	96.71	88.89	82.61	1.69	0.03	84.51	83.33	86.96	3.19	0.06	99.60	96.83	81.99	0.04	0.37	97.65	88.89	90.06
11	21.00	0.01	73.40	54.55	37.21	1.67	0.00	0.00	0.00	0.00	3.19	0.11	64.45	40.91	37.21	0.19	0.67	47.61	31.82	39.53
12	18.00	0.01	94.69	60.00	82.35	1.67	0.00	0.00	0.00	0.00	3.14	0.01	1.77	0.00	0.00	0.30	0.01	0.00	0.00	0.00
13	13.00	0.01	100.00	87.50	86.36	1.71	0.15	89.92	87.50	72.73	3.17	0.08	100.00	94.64	90.91	0.03	0.33	76.47	43.75	63.64
14	17.00	0.01	100.00	0.00	100.00	1.68	0.01	100.00	0.00	50.00	3.13	0.01	100.00	0.00	50.00	0.02	0.07	100.00	0.00	50.00
15	22.00	0.01	52.42	66.67	40.00	1.67	0.00	0.00	0.00	0.00	3.27	0.07	98.30	91.27	60.00	0.05	0.33	79.30	61.11	45.71
16	20.00	0.01	43.62	45.83	50.79	1.69	0.05	49.73	47.92	52.38	3.30	0.18	100.00	95.83	81.86	0.05	0.59	80.32	41.67	68.25
17	10.00	0.01	53.05	46.30	33.78	1.68	0.01	49.05	35.19	25.68	3.30	0.17	95.47	88.36	57.14	0.08	0.64	81.49	48.15	61.78
18	22.00	0.01	49.42	52.78	41.33	1.69	0.06	56.59	52.78	49.33	3.24	0.14	93.91	91.27	68.76	0.09	0.62	82.17	58.33	76.00
19	17.00	0.03	27.96	24.51	22.86	1.67	0.00	0.00	0.00	0.00	6.73	0.04	0.16	6.16	3.54	0.02	0.00	0.00	0.00	0.00
20	30.00	0.01	53.11	44.90	54.22	1.69	0.03	59.52	41.84	55.42	3.40	0.24	78.15	70.12	17.56	0.19	0.65	59.59	33.67	36.83
21	15.00	0.15	4.07	12.50	1.08	1.67	0.00	0.00	0.00	0.00	2.75	0.06	1.11	3.90	0.36	6.01	0.00	0.00	0.00	0.00
22	30.00	0.02	44.47	35.71	41.54	1.69	0.07	39.86	25.00	0.00	9.02	0.00	0.00	0.00	0.00	0.22	1.05	49.54	27.38	21.54
23	20.00	0.01	78.92	43.33	19.09	1.67	0.00	0.00	0.00	0.00	8.71	0.11	39.76	27.62	32.34	0.03	0.00	0.00	0.00	0.00
24	10.00	0.01	56.33	50.94	44.44	1.68	0.01	88.60	65.63	73.59	3.35	0.24	74.62	67.25	68.69	0.09	0.71	89.47	86.79	87.59
25	15.00	0.01	53.82	46.51	39.53	1.69	0.01	86.68	63.95	73.26	3.31	0.24	72.77	67.11	65.95	0.09	0.71	87.11	84.55	86.05
26	30.00	0.01	81.81	41.53	54.24	1.67	0.00	0.00	0.00	0.00	3.43	0.28	92.98	64.65	70.09	0.13	0.70	31.48	21.19	29.17
27	13.00	0.01	38.78	24.59	23.93	1.67	0.00	0.00	0.00	0.00	8.59	0.09	23.76	21.31	16.83	0.02	0.00	0.00	0.00	0.00
28	19.00	0.02	29.68	29.51	15.65	1.68	0.00	0.00	0.00	0.00	2.70	0.00	0.00	0.00	0.00	9.35	0.01	4.24	4.22	1.69
29	25.00	0.01	30.92	31.71	37.50	1.67	0.00	0.00	0.00	0.00	3.45	0.22	85.90	80.49	59.07	2.59	0.01	0.00	0.00	0.00
30	20.00	0.01	52.43	40.00	43.69	1.71	0.21	92.48	77.14	0.14	3.30	0.17	98.97	67.55	56.59	0.07	0.59	51.16	31.43	50.49
31	16.00	0.01	39.95	34.09	28.26	1.67	0.01	5.21	0.00	0.00	3.36	0.06	53.31	43.83	46.27	0.07	0.08	3.62	0.00	2.17
32	13.00	0.01	39.41	41.89	20.00	1.69	0.03	21.19	9.46	26.67	3.79	0.17	62.98	59.46	36.43	0.35	1.23	57.25	45.75	34.76
33	10.00	0.01	12.66	11.36	15.00	1.69	0.05	16.89	9.09	27.50	4.37	0.09	46.85	37.01	36.07	0.08	0.80	56.99	50.00	47.50
34	9.00	0.01	25.97	25.00	16.67	1.71	0.18	15.58	0.00	25.00	4.13	0.15	83.55	81.12	67.26	0.08	0.63	62.34	42.86	41.67
35	20.00	0.01	22.43	22.73	19.13	1.69	0.02	27.24	15.91	23.48	3.47	0.23	42.59	30.84	33.04	0.38	1.23	46.45	37.01	43.73
36	17.00	0.01	63.21	57.07	48.60	1.67	0.00	0.00	0.00	0.00	6.96	0.07	70.86	65.00	47.73	0.31	1.06	20.47	7.33	5.03
37	15.00	0.01	61.80	65.22	46.81	1.69	0.02	60.52	60.87	57.45	3.30	0.09	84.40	90.06	77.20	0.20	0.69	49.14	34.78	0.00
38	11.00	0.01	60.30	61.11	45.95	1.68	0.01	30.34	38.89	24.32	3.24	0.12	96.20	79.37	96.14	0.08	0.17	32.10	43.65	29.34
39	30.00	0.01	37.40	27.08	25.66	1.69	0.01	29.09	6.25	10.62	3.31	0.13	36.90	19.35	22.63	0.18	0.60	34.42	8.33	16.81
40	12.00	0.01	63.46	46.15	20.83	1.67	0.00	0.00	0.00	0.00	3.22	0.02	55.77	30.77	26.79	0.07	0.19	39.42	19.23	22.32
41	17.00	0.01	84.86	73.08	67.03	1.69	0.02	79.04	71.15	59.34	3.24	0.11	93.74	87.91	82.89	0.12	0.63	40.49	7.97	20.88
42	9.00	0.01	78.01	54.17	59.09	1.69	0.01	21.99	8.33	11.36	3.18	0.04	30.03	21.43	27.60	0.08	0.07	8.90	0.00	6.82
43	10.00	0.01	89.25	66.67	65.38	1.67	0.00	0.00	0.00	0.00	8.24	0.00	0.00	0.00	0.00	0.37	0.01	0.00	0.00	0.00
44	45.00	0.01	91.33	77.14	69.75	1.67	0.00	0.00	0.00	0.00	3.09	0.01	21.41	20.71	27.73	0.09	0.05	14.80	14.29	3.36
45	20.00	0.03	0.00	0.00	0.00	1.67	0.00	0.00	0.00	0.00	2.81	0.01	0.64	2.00	1.90	0.48	0.01	46.04	0.00	0.00
46	26.00	0.01	49.01	42.86	45.83	1.67	0.00	0.00	0.00	0.00	3.14	0.05	46.55	40.82	34.23	0.08	0.34	46.04	36.05	36.31
47	20.00	0.01	45.36	18.60	2.22	1.67	0.00	0.00	0.00	0.00	2.62	0.03	14.93	7.31	0.00	0.08	0.01	0.00	0.00	0.00
48	10.00	0.01	89.51	87.50	50.00	1.72	0.18	58.64	62.50	85.71	3.16	0.03	76.01	76.79	92.86	0.03	0.49	57.41	50.00	50.00
49	35.00	0.01	24.93	18.00	20.90	1.67	0.00	0.00	0.00	0.00	3.19	0.07	10.78	10.29	12.58	6.01	0.00	0.00	0.00	0.00
50	21.68	0.01	62.00	25.00	30.00	1.67	0.00	0.00	0.00	0.00	3.30	0.01	77.00	50.00	18.57	0.04	0.00	0.00	0.00	0.00
51	74.13	0.01	88.44	86.67	100.00	1.67	0.00	0.00	0.00	0.00	3.24	0.10	58.11	54.29	46.75	0.05	0.08	20.41	16.67	18.18
52	38.72	0.01	55.24	57.14	20.93	1.67	0.01	0.53	0.00	0.00	4.45	0.02	49.45	29.59	13.29	0.05	0.32	44.76	21.43	13.95
53	31.87	0.01	76.88	38.46	42.00	1.70	0.10	82.17	61.54	66.00	3.35	0.10	59.57	53.30	50.29	0.09	0.71	71.71	53.30	54.86
54	47.68	0.01	81.60	73.08	61.70	1.67	0.00	0.00	0.00	0.00	3.43	0.09	48.53	45.60	55.93	0.54	0.08	17.60	11.54	10.64
55	68.35	0.01	77.22	51.00	60.66	1.67	0.00	0.00	0.00	0.00	6.15	0.04	48.73	33.29	10.07	0.03	0.35	25.63	11.00	29.51
56	42.32	0.01	96.36	92.31	90.48	1.68	0.01	54.25	61.54	61.90	3.49	0.13	55.75	78.02	62.31	0.04	0.50	74.73	71.43	68.03
57	20.73	0.01	97.02	92.86	65.63	1.67	0.00	0.00	0.00	0.00	3.69	0.08	87.06	67.86	69.08	0.04	0.35	86.67	70.41	71.88
58	26.17	0.01	100.00	0.00	74.19	1.68	0.01	100.00	0.00	93.55	3.18	0.08	100.00	0.00	47.33	0.04	0.53	100.00	0.00	0.00
59	28.40	0.01	95.76	90.00	53.23	1.69	0.00	0.00	0.00	0.00	3.30	0.10	95.04	97.14	60.60	0.16	0.55	0.00	0.00	0.00
60	24.77	0.01	87.50	87.50	67.74	1.69	0.02	94.57	87.50	0.00	4.07	0.15	98.84	98.66	76.73	0.76	1.31	84.08	56.25	67.74
61	17.20	0.01	86.39	80.00	56.25	1.67	0.00	0.00	0.00	0.00	3.26	0.16	87.56	82.86	80.36	0.22	0.74	39.99	40.00	59.38
62	53.58	0.01	91.86	81.25	64.71	1.69	0.02	94.88	75.00	0.00	3.32	0.16	98.17	87.50	72.90	0.34	1.10	91.86	62.50	77.52
63	9.00	0.01	97.46	100.00	50.00	1.67	0.00	2.54	0.00	0.00	3.15	0.01	0.00	0.00	0.00	0.03	0.09	36.44	25.00	16.67

	Manual	Randoop	EvoSuite	T3
Files	63.00	207.43	777.43	3385.71
Instructions	16006.86 / 32917 (48.63%)	6821.86 / 32917 (20.72%)	15555.57 / 32917 (47.26 %)	9830.71 / 32917 (29.87%)
Branches	1145.00 / 2555 (44.81%)	494.57 / 2555 (19.36%)	1252.86 / 2555 (49.04 %)	653.43 / 2555 (25.57%)
Mutants	1499.00 / 3903 (38.41%)	585.00 / 3903 (14.99%)	1555.86 / 3903 (39.86 %)	1041.43 / 3903 (26.68%)
CB Mutations	71.14 / 195 (36.48%)	20.00 / 195 (10.26%)	83.57 / 195 (42.86 %)	47.00 / 195 (24.10%)
NC Mutations	572.86 / 1252 (45.76%)	198.00 / 1252 (15.81%)	530.71 / 1252 (42.39 %)	322.86 / 1252 (25.79%)
M Mutations	120.00 / 334 (35.93%)	40.00 / 334 (11.98%)	144.00 / 334 (43.11 %)	131.71 / 334 (39.43%)
I Mutations	69.00 / 101 (68.32%)	7.00 / 101 (6.93%)	64.86 / 101 (64.21 %)	23.14 / 101 (22.91%)
IN Mutations	3.00 / 6 (50.00%)	1.00 / 6 (16.67%)	1.71 / 6 (28.57 %)	2.00 / 6 (33.33%)
RV Mutations	605.86 / 1576 (38.44%)	294.00 / 1576 (18.65%)	656.00 / 1576 (41.62 %)	430.71 / 1576 (27.33%)
VMC Mutations	57.14 / 439 (13.02%)	25.00 / 439 (5.69%)	75.00 / 439 (17.08 %)	84.00 / 439 (19.13%)
Avg. cov_i	67.78%	31.58%	59.90%	44.81%
Avg. cov_b	50.90%	19.02%	48.63%	26.68%
Avg. cov_m	50.21%	20.39%	43.80%	33.38%
Avg. t_{gen}	21.83 m	1.68 m	3.83 m	31.32 s
Avg. t_{exec}	0.01 m	1.61 s	5.19 s	24.96 s
Total t_{gen}	22.92 h	1.77 h	4.03 h	32.88 m
Total t_{exec}	0.72 m	1.69 m	5.45 m	26.20 m
Score	210.45	93.45	205.26	144.98

times in order to obtain an average value for the measured variables. However, due to time and resource restrictions we could only run each tool a maximum of six or seven times, respectively. This could have affected the accuracy of our results.

3. Another threat might occur regarding the manual baseline of the contest. In the second round of the competition, the testers that wrote unit tests have not been the authors of any of the CUTs. This means that they might have spent more time on creating tests, since they had to get familiar with the relevant classes. Often this also includes classes that the CUTs depend on which can consume additional time.

Internal Validity. The following threats could affect the interpretability of the findings:

1. Artifacts used in the study: This is the effect caused by the artifacts used for (experiment) competition execution, such as selected CUTs and seeded mutants. Our study could be affected negatively if both artifacts (CUTs and seeded mutants) were not selected appropriately. Other artifacts used for this study were the benchmark-tool and the run tools that were specifically developed for this competition. To ensure a good performance of the benchmark-tool, it was previously tested by the benchmark developer. With respect to the run-tools implemented by each participant, they were also tested to tune their tools' parameters, by using practice-benchmarks, compiled from popular open source projects, that were not part of the final competition.

Construct Validity. This relates to the admissibility of statements about the underlying constructs on the basis of the operationalization. The following threat has been identified:

1. Inadequate pre-operational Explication of Constructs: In our study, the final score has been calculated based on a benchmark function whose weights were assigned in accordance with those quality indicators that are considered most important. The weights were chosen based on the experience gained through empirical studies evaluating other testing tools in industry. Most of these studies conclude that for companies the most important characteristics of a testing tool are (1) to find errors (mutation coverage) (2) quickly (time).

5 Conclusion

This paper describes the two rounds of the competition that we have executed for automated Java unit testing tools. Preparing for the competition, looking for participants and making everything work has been quite a challenging endeavour. However, looking at the results and the enthusiasm with which the tool developers received the scores and learned from the results, it was also a very awarding experience.

After the first round we improved several aspects of the framework and learned a lot about carrying out such a benchmark. There are a few aspects, however, that we will dedicate time to in future benchmarks:

- We improved the benchmark framework which now works with Java 7 and is more reliable than the first version. However, measuring the variables for all CUTs and tools still takes a considerable amount of time, so we will continue to improve the implementation to make the process more efficient.

– After discussions with the participants, we changed the benchmark formula in order to emphasize the importance of achieved mutation score and reduce the impact of generation time. However, we think that the benchmark formula and the values of its weights are likely to be adapted in future competitions as we will continue to discuss with he participants. One of the ideas is to have several scores for different aspects of the tools, such as code coverage only and mutation coverage only.

– The amount of participants: We plan to spread the word and make the competition more popular, so that more tool developers from research as well as industry will participate and improve the state of the art. One way to achieve this, might be to change the benchmark protocol. Currently, tools which need to instrument the entire project in order to generate tests, have a significant disadvantage, since they do not know the CUTs ahead of time and might thus spend too much time on instrumentation. In fact, in the second competition, the protocol prevented several potential participants from implementing a run tool. A protocol which gives more freedom with regard to the order of test generation and which presents the entire set of CUTs all at once, instead of as a sequence of chunks, might reflect a more realistic test setting and could encourage more developers to participate.

– Contrary to the last competition, where we only used unit tests written by the developers of the CUTs, we wrote our own unit tests this time. We measured the time to create these tests and where thus able to assign a benchmark score. This made it possible to use the tests as a direct baseline and allowed interesting comparisons to be made with the automated solutions. The tool developers were able to analyse where their tools need improvement and where they are up to par or even exceed the human tester. However, we only had three different testers that wrote the manual test cases. Ideally, in the next event, we will have more testers and a greater amount and variety of CUTs in order to make the competition as realistic as possible.

Acknowledgements. This work is funded by the European Project with the acronym FITTEST (Future Internet Testing) and contract number (ICT-257574). We would also like to thank Arthur Baars for his initial efforts in setting up the benchmark architecture.

References

1. Apache Commons Lang v3.1. http://commons.apache.org/lang. Accessed 22 Feb 2013
2. Apache Lucene v4.1.0. http://lucene.apache.org. Accessed 22 Feb 2013
3. Async Http Client v1.7.20. https://github.com/AsyncHttpClient/async-http-client. Accessed 03 Sept 2013
4. Barbecue v1.5 beta. http://barbecue.sourceforge.net. Accessed 22 Feb 2013
5. Cobertura v1.9.4.1. http://cobertura.sourceforge.net. Accessed 22 Feb 2013
6. Eclipse checkstyle plugin v5.6.1. http://eclipse-cs.sourceforge.net/. Accessed 2 Sept 2013

7. Gdata Java Client v1.4.7.1. https://code.google.com/p/gdata-java-client/. Accessed 8 July 2013
8. Guava v15. https://code.google.com/p/guava-libraries/. Accessed 8 Sept 2013
9. Hibernate v4.2.7. http://www.hibernate.org. Accessed 2 Sept 2013
10. JaCoCo v0.6.3. http://www.eclemma.org/jacoco/. Accessed 24 Oct 2013
11. Java Machine Learning Libraryr v0.1.7. http://java-ml.sourceforge.net/. Accessed 9 Sept 2013
12. Java Wikipedia Library v0.9.2. https://code.google.com/p/jwpl/. Accessed 17 July 2013
13. Joda Time v2.0. http://joda-time.sourceforge.net. Accessed 22 Feb 2013
14. Pitest v0.3.1. http://pitest.org. Accessed 24 Oct 2013
15. Randoop v1.3.3. http://code.google.com/p/randoop/. Accessed 22 Feb 2013
16. Scribe v1.3.5. https://github.com/fernandezpablo85/scribe-java. Accessed 3 Sept 2013
17. sqlsheet v6.4. https://code.google.com/p/sqlsheet. Accessed 22 Feb 2013
18. Twitter4j v3.0.4. http://twitter4j.org/en/. Accessed 3 Sept 2013
19. Andrews, J., Menzies, T., Li, F.: Genetic algorithms for randomized unit testing. IEEE Trans. Softw. Eng. **37**(1), 80–94 (2011)
20. Basili, V.R., Shull, F., Lanubile, F.: Building knowledge through families of experiments. IEEE Trans. Softw. Eng. **25**(4), 456–473 (1999)
21. Daniel, B., Boshernitsan, M.: Predicting effectiveness of automatic testing tools. In: 23rd IEEE/ACM International Conference on Automated Software Engineering 2008, ASE 2008, pp. 363–366 (2008)
22. Fraser, G., Zeller, A.: Mutation-driven generation of unit tests and oracles. IEEE Trans. Softw. Eng **38**(2), 278–292 (2012)
23. Fraser, G., Arcuri, A.: Sound empirical evidence in software testing. In: Proceedings of the 2012 International Conference on Software Engineering, ICSE 2012, pp. 178–188. IEEE Press, Piscataway (2012). http://dl.acm.org/citation.cfm?id=2337223.2337245
24. Fraser, G., Arcuri, A.: Evosuite at the SBST 2013 tool competition. In: 2013 IEEE Sixth International Conference on Software Testing, Verification and Validation Workshops (ICSTW), pp. 406–409, March 2013
25. Fraser, G., Arcuri, A.: Evosuite at the second unit testing tool competition. In: Future Internet Testing (FITTEST) Workshop (2014)
26. Harman, M., Jia, Y., Langdon, W.B.: Strong higher order mutation-based test data generation. In: Gyimóthy, T., Zeller, A. (eds.) SIGSOFT FSE. pp. 212–222. ACM (2011). http://doi.acm.org/10.1145/2025113.2025144
27. Kitchenham, B., Dyba, T., Jorgensen, M.: Evidence-based software engineering. In: Proceedings of ICSE, pp. 273–281. IEEE (2004)
28. Kitchenham, B.A., Pfleeger, S.L., Pickard, L.M., Jones, P.W., Hoaglin, D.C., Emam, K.E., Rosenberg, J.: Preliminary guidelines for empirical research in software engineering. IEEE Trans. Softw. Eng. **28**(8), 721–734 (2002)
29. Nistor, A., Luo, Q., Pradel, M., Gross, T., Marinov, D.: Ballerina: Automatic generation and clustering of efficient random unit tests for multithreaded code. In: 2012 34th International Conference on Software Engineering (ICSE), pp. 727–737, June 2012
30. Pacheco, C., Ernst, M.D.: Randoop: feedback-directed random testing for java. In: Companion to the 22nd ACM SIGPLAN Conference on Object-Oriented Programming Systems and Applications Companion, OOPSLA '07, pp. 815–816. ACM, New York (2007). http://doi.acm.org/10.1145/1297846.1297902

31. Pacheco, C., Lahiri, S.K., Ball, T.: Finding errors in.net with feedback-directed random testing. In: Proceedings of the 2008 International Symposium on Software Testing and Analysis, ISSTA '08, pp. 87–96. ACM, New York (2008). http://doi.acm.org/10.1145/1390630.1390643

32. Prasetya, I.: Measuring T2 against SBST 2013 benchmark suite. In: 2013 IEEE Sixth International Conference on Software Testing, Verification and Validation Workshops (ICSTW), pp. 410–413, March 2013

33. Prasetya, I.: T3, a combinator-based random testing tool for java: benchmarking. In: Future Internet Testing (FITTEST) Workshop (2014)

34. Schuler, D., Zeller, A.: Javalanche: efficient mutation testing for java. In: ESEC/FSE '09: Proceedings of the 7th Joint Meeting of the European Software Engineering Conference and the ACM SIGSOFT International Symposium on Foundations of Software Engineering, pp. 297–298, Aug 2009

35. Schuler, D., Zeller, A.: (un-)covering equivalent mutants. In: ICST '10: Proceedings of the 3rd International Conference on Software Testing, Verification and Validation, pp. 45–54. IEEE Computer Society, Apr 2010

36. Sim, S., Easterbrook, S., Holt, R.: Using benchmarking to advance research: a challenge to software engineering. In: Proceedings of the 25th International Conference on Software Engineering, 2003, pp. 74–83, May 2003

37. Tonella, P., Torchiano, M., Du Bois, B., Systä, T.: Empirical studies in reverse engineering: state of the art and future trends. Empirical Softw. Engg. **12**(5), 551–571 (2007)

38. Vegas, S., Basili, V.: A characterisation schema for software testing techniques. Empirical Softw. Engg. **10**(4), 437–466 (2005)

EvoSuite at the Second Unit Testing Tool Competition

Gordon Fraser[1]([✉]) and Andrea Arcuri[2]

[1] Department of Computer Science, University of Sheffield, Sheffield, UK
gordon.fraser@sheffield.ac.uk
[2] Simula Research Laboratory, P.O. Box 134, 1325 Lysaker, Norway
arcuri@simula.no

Abstract. EVOSUITE is a mature research prototype implementing a search-based approach to unit test generation for Java classes. It has been successfully run on a variety of different Java projects in the past, and after winning the first instance of the unit testing tool competition at SBST'13, it has also taken part in the second run. This paper reports on the obstacles and challenges encountered during the latter competition.

Keywords: Automated unit testing · Search-based testing · Competition

1 Introduction

The EVOSUITE test generation tool is a mature research prototype that automatically generates unit test suites for given Java classes. The first experiments with EVOSUITE were reported in [3], and it has since been applied to a range of different projects and domains [4,9], leading to various improvements over time. In the first unit test competition organised at the SBST'13 workshop [2], EVOSUITE obtained the highest score among the participating tools [8].

Besides the obvious research challenge of achieving high coverage, the challenges in building a tool like EVOSUITE often lie in practical issues imposed by the Java language, and the nature of real code. For example, often the structure of code is trivial in terms of the complexity of the branching conditions, yet difficult for a testing tool as the code has complex environmental dependencies, such as files and databases [5]. These findings are once more confirmed by the results of the second unit testing tool competition. In this paper, we analyze the major obstacles EVOSUITE encountered in this second competition by focusing on classes where the coverage is particularly low.

2 About EVOSUITE

EVOSUITE is a tool that automatically produces unit test suites for Java classes with the aim to maximize code coverage. As input it requires only the bytecode

T.E.J. Vos, K. Lakhotia, and S. Bauersfeld (Eds.): FITTEST 2013, LNCS 8432, pp. 95–100, 2014.
DOI: 10.1007/978-3-319-07785-7_6, © Springer International Publishing Switzerland 2014

Table 1. Description of EvoSuite

Prerequisites	
Static or dynamic	Dynamic testing at the Java class level
Software type	Java classes
Lifecycle phase	Unit testing for Java programs
Environment	All Java development environments
Knowledge required	JUnit unit testing for Java
Experience required	Basic unit testing knowledge
Input and output of the tool	
Input	Bytecode of the target class and dependencies
Output	JUnit test cases (version 3 or 4)
Operation	
Interaction	Through the command line
User guidance	manual verification of assertions for functional faults
Source of information	http://www.evosuite.org
Maturity	Mature research prototype, under development
Technology behind the tool	Search-based testing/whole test suite generation
Obtaining the tool and information	
License	GNU General Public License V3
Cost	Open source
Support	None
Empirical evidence about the tool	
Effectiveness and scalability	See [4,9]

of the class under test as well as its dependencies. This is provided automatically when using the Eclipse-frontend to interact with EvoSuite, and on the command-line it amounts to setting a classpath and specifying the target class name as a command-line parameter.

EvoSuite applies a search-based approach, where a genetic algorithm optimizes whole test suites towards a chosen target criterion (e.g., branch coverage by default). The advantage of this approach is that it is not negatively affected by infeasible goals and its performance does not depend on the order in which testing goals are considered, as has been demonstrated in the past [9]. To increase the performance further, EvoSuite integrates dynamic symbolic execution (DSE) in a hybrid approach [11], where primitive values (e.g., numbers or strings) are optimized using a constraint solver. However, due to the experimental nature of this feature it was not activated during the competition.

The search-based optimization in EvoSuite results in a set of sequences of method calls that maximizes coverage, yet these sequences are not yet usable as unit test cases — at least not for human consumption. In order to make it easier to understand and use the test cases produced, EvoSuite applies a range of post-processing steps to produce sets of small and concise unit tests. The final step of this post-processing consists of adding test assertions, i.e., statements that check the outcome of the test. As EVOSUITE only requires the bytecode as input and such bytecode often does not include formal specifications, the assertions produced will reflect observed behavior, rather than the intended behavior. Consequently, the test cases are intended either as regression tests, or serve as starting point for a human tester, who can manually revise the assertions in order to determine failures [10]. However, EVOSUITE is also able to automatically detect certain classes of bugs which are independent of a specification; for example, undeclared exceptions or violations of assertions in the code [6].

Table 1 describes EVOSUITE in terms of the template used in the unit testing tool competition.

3   Configuration for the Competition Entry

Even though several new features have been developed for EVOSUITE (e.g., DSE integration [11]) since the last competition, we did not include any for the competition entry, as the risk of reducing the score due to immature code would be too high. One notable new feature we did include because it is now enabled by default is support for Java Generics [7]. Besides this, the version of EVOSUITE used in the competition is largely the same as in the first round in terms of features, yet has seen many revisions to fix individual problems or bugs.

We used the same configuration as for the first unit testing competition without any changes. This means that EVOSUITE was configured to optimize for weak mutation testing, with three minutes time for the search per class. Minimization was deactivated to reduce the test generation time, and EVOSUITE was configured to include all possible assertions in the tests (rather than the default of minimizing the assertions using mutation analysis [10]). For all other parameters, EVOSUITE was configured to its default parameter settings [1].

4   Results and Problems

Coverage results achieved by EVOSUITE are listed in Table 2. On the 63 classes of the benchmark used in the competition, EVOSUITE produced an average instruction coverage of 59.9 %, average branch coverage of 48.63 %, and average mutation score of 43.8 %. These results are in line with our expectations based on recent experimentation [4].

For each class it produced on average 12.3 test cases. For the entire benchmark of 63 classes, EVOSUITE took on average 4 h for test generation, which means that EVOSUITE spent an additional 51 s per class on the up-front analysis of the classpath as well as the post-processing after the search.

In the following discussion, we focus on some interesting cases where EVO-SUITE achieved no or very little (<2 %) coverage or mutation score.

Trivial classes: Class 1 (*SearchException*) is a trivial class with only 15 lines of code, and it seems surprising that EVOSUITE achieved 0 % coverage here. The reason for this bad result is that the class consists of four constructors

Table 2. EvoSuite results on the benchmark classes

No.	Class	Project	LOC	NBD	Time (min)		Coverage		
					Gen	Exec	Instr.	Branch	Mutation
1	SearchException	Hibernate	15	1	3.23	0.00	0.00	0.00	0.00
2	Version	Hibernate	12	1	3.74	0.01	60.00	0.00	0.00
3	BackendFactory	Hibernate	72	2	4.53	0.02	27.71	6.25	40.95
4	FlushLuceneWork	Hibernate	26	2	3.22	0.03	89.74	100.00	75.00
5	OptimizeLuceneWork	Hibernate	26	2	3.22	0.03	89.74	100.00	75.00
6	LoggerFactory	Hibernate	14	1	7.75	0.01	17.41	0.00	0.00
7	LoggerHelper	Hibernate	17	1	3.73	0.01	87.50	0.00	33.33
8	OAuthConfig	Scribe	63	3	3.21	0.05	91.14	100.00	100.00
9	OAuthRequest	Scribe	36	2	3.15	0.03	100.00	100.00	80.00
10	ParameterList	Scribe	95	3	3.19	0.06	99.60	96.83	81.99
11	Request	Scribe	213	2	3.19	0.11	64.45	40.91	37.21
12	Response	Scribe	72	2	3.14	0.01	1.77	0.00	0.00
13	Token	Scribe	64	2	3.17	0.08	100.00	94.64	90.91
14	Verifier	Scribe	15	1	3.13	0.01	100.00	0.00	50.00
15	ExceptionDiagnosis	Twitter4j	73	4	3.27	0.07	98.30	91.27	60.00
16	GeoQuery	Twitter4j	126	2	3.30	0.18	100.00	95.83	81.86
17	OEmbedRequest	Twitter4j	147	2	3.30	0.17	95.47	88.36	57.14
18	Paging	Twitter4j	171	3	3.24	0.14	93.91	91.27	68.76
19	TwitterBaseImpl	Twitter4j	328	5	6.73	0.04	9.16	6.16	3.54
20	TwitterException	Twitter4j	237	4	3.40	0.24	78.15	70.12	17.56
21	TwitterImpl	Twitter4j	1187	3	2.75	0.06	1.11	3.90	0.36
22	AsyncHttpClient	Async Http Client	296	5	9.02	0.00	0.00	0.00	0.00
23	AsyncHttpClientConfig	Async Http Client	621	2	8.71	0.11	39.76	27.62	32.34
24	FluentCaseInsensitiveStringsMap	Async Http Client	292	4	3.35	0.24	74.62	67.25	68.69
25	FluentStringsMap	Async Http Client	240	4	3.31	0.24	72.77	67.11	65.95
26	Realm	Async Http Client	481	3	3.43	0.28	92.98	64.65	70.09
27	RequestBuilderBase	Async Http Client	544	6	8.59	0.09	23.76	21.31	16.83
28	SimpleAsyncHttpClient	Async Http Client	610	3	2.70	0.00	0.00	0.00	0.00
29	AttributeHelper	GData Java Client	344	4	3.45	0.22	85.90	80.49	59.07
30	DateTime	GData Java Client	264	5	3.30	0.19	78.97	67.55	56.59
31	Kind	GData Java Client	189	5	3.36	0.06	53.31	43.83	46.27
32	Link	GData Java Client	190	4	3.79	0.17	62.98	59.46	36.43
33	OtherContent	GData Java Client	179	4	4.37	0.09	46.85	37.01	36.07
34	OutOfLineContent	GData Java Client	102	4	4.13	0.15	83.55	81.12	67.26
35	Source	GData Java Client	324	4	3.47	0.23	42.59	30.84	33.04
36	CharMatcher	Guava	824	4	6.96	0.07	70.86	65.00	47.73
37	Joiner	Guava	222	3	3.30	0.09	84.40	90.06	77.20
38	Objects	Guava	130	4	3.24	0.12	96.20	79.37	96.14
39	Predicates	Guava	379	3	3.31	0.13	36.99	19.35	22.63
40	SmallCharMatcher	Guava	92	4	3.22	0.02	55.77	30.77	26.79
41	Splitter	Guava	266	4	3.24	0.11	93.74	87.91	82.89
42	Suppliers	Guava	172	4	3.18	0.04	30.03	21.43	27.60
43	CategoryDescendantsIterator	JWPL	103	4	3.18	0.01	8.24	0.00	0.00
44	CycleHandler	JWPL	71	4	3.09	0.01	21.41	20.71	27.73
45	Page	JWPL	351	4	2.81	0.01	0.64	2.00	1.90
46	PageIterator	JWPL	182	7	3.14	0.05	46.55	40.82	34.23
47	PageQueryIterable	JWPL	131	3	2.62	0.03	14.93	7.31	0.00
48	Title	JWPL	79	2	3.16	0.03	76.01	76.79	92.86
49	WikipediaInfo	JWPL	222	6	3.19	0.07	10.78	10.29	12.58
50	AbstractLoader	eclipse-cs	77	3	3.30	0.01	77.00	50.00	18.57
51	AnnotationUtility	eclipse-cs	78	4	3.24	0.10	58.11	54.29	46.75
52	AutomaticBean	eclipse-cs	178	4	4.45	0.02	49.45	29.59	13.29
53	FileContents	eclipse-cs	161	4	3.35	0.10	59.57	53.30	50.29
54	FileText	eclipse-cs	184	4	3.43	0.09	48.53	45.60	55.93
55	ScopeUtils	eclipse-cs	189	4	6.15	0.04	48.73	33.29	10.07
56	Utils	eclipse-cs	160	4	3.49	0.13	55.75	78.02	65.31
57	AbstractInstance	JMLL	136	2	3.69	0.08	87.06	67.86	68.08
58	Complex	JMLL	53	1	3.18	0.08	100.00	0.00	47.93
59	DefaultDataset	JMLL	152	3	3.30	0.10	95.04	97.14	60.60
60	DenseInstance	JMLL	155	3	4.07	0.15	98.84	98.66	76.73
61	Fold	JMLL	201	2	3.26	0.16	87.56	82.86	80.36
62	SparseInstance	JMLL	191	3	3.32	0.16	98.17	87.50	72.90
63	ARFFHandler	JMLL	51	6	3.15	0.01	0.00	0.00	0.00

that do nothing but calling the constructor of the superclass, and as a result there are no statements for which EvoSuite produced any mutants, and there are no branching instructions. While the standard branch coverage criterion in EvoSuite also enforces that each method is executed at least once, the weak mutation testing criterion we used in the competition did not do so at the time of the competition, and so EvoSuite produced no tests.

Classpath dependent behavior: Class 2 (*Version*) is another trivial class, yet the reason for the bad result do not lie in EvoSuite, but rather the frontend of EvoSuite we built to interface with the competition infrastructure. When setting up the classpath for EvoSuite, our competition frontend unnecessarily included the source directory of the unit under test in the classpath. In the competition setup there are compiled versions of the classes in the source directory as well as a dedicated target path; unfortunately, they differ: Method *getVersionString* returns "[WORKING]" in the class in the source directory, whereas the deployed version of the class is changed to return "[0.4.4-SNAPSHOT]". As EvoSuite's assertions were expecting "[WORKING]", resulting tests failed and were not considered for mutation analysis.

Nondeterministic code: Class 30 (*DateTime*) makes use of the current system time, such that automatically generated assertions may refer to the time of test execution. If this happens, then the tests will fail, and will not be considered for mutation analysis. This is a known issue, and EvoSuite overcomes it by using bytecode instrumentation that replaces nondeterministic calls. However, as the PIT mutation testing tool used in the competition is not able to handle JUnit tests with this kind of instrumentation, we had to deactivate it. EvoSuite does compile and execute tests as a last step to comment out any failing assertions; yet in this case there were assertions dependent on the seconds of the current time, and so this verification step was too quick to notice the failing assertions.

Environmental dependencies: One of the largest problems in unit testing remains the handling of environmental dependencies. For example, most classes in the JWPL project (43–49) depend on a valid instance of a *Wikipedia* class, which in turn depends on a valid *DatabaseConfiguration*. As another example, class 63 (ARFFHandler) consists of only one method (and one wrapper for that method) that receives a file as parameter, and then tries to parse this file.

Complex classes: The benchmark included large classes, most notably class 21 (*TwitterImpl*): This class has 1,187 lines of code, and EvoSuite produced 2,453 mutants for it. That on its own would not be a challenge for EvoSuite; however, test execution on this class turns out to be very slow, and can lead to excessive memory consumption. To prevent out of memory exceptions from occurring and crashing EvoSuite, EvoSuite cancels test generation when the Java garbage collector fails to free sufficient memory. This happened not only in this class, but also several others (19, 23, 43, 44, 45, 47, 49). Running EvoSuite with more memory would have likely resulted in higher coverage on these classes.

5 Conclusions

With an overall score of 205.26, EvoSuite achieved the highest score of all tools in the competition. The score calculated for manual testing is 210.45 — a very close call. This means that EvoSuite is achieving almost human-competitive results in terms of the effectiveness of the resulting test suites. Potentially, just by fixing some of the errors in EvoSuite or its competition frontend the resulting score could be higher than 210, even without adding new features. We are confident that some of the experimental features will further increase this once the required level of robustness has been achieved.

Acknowledgments. This project has been funded by a Google Focused Research Award on "Test Amplification" and the Norwegian Research Council.

References

1. Arcuri, A., Fraser, G.: Parameter tuning or default values? An empirical investigation in search-based software engineering. Empirical Softw. Eng. (EMSE), 1–30 (2013)
2. Bauersfeld, S., Vos, T., Lakhotia, K., Poulding, S., Condori, N.: Unit testing tool competition. In: International Workshop on Search-Based Software Testing (SBST), pp. 414–420 (2013)
3. Fraser, G., Arcuri, A.: Evolutionary generation of whole test suites. In: International Conference on Quality Software (QSIC), pp. 31–40. IEEE Computer Society (2011)
4. Fraser, G., Arcuri, A.: Sound empirical evidence in software testing. In: ACM/IEEE International Conference on Software Engineering (ICSE), pp. 178–188 (2012)
5. Fraser, G., Arcuri, A.: EvoSuite: on the challenges of test case generation in the real world (tool paper). In: IEEE International Conference on Software Testing, Verification and Validation (ICST) (2013)
6. Fraser, G., Arcuri, A.: 1600 faults in 100 projects: automatically finding faults while achieving high coverage with evosuite. Empirical Softw. Eng. (to appear, 2013)
7. Fraser, Gordon, Arcuri, Andrea: Automated test generation for Java generics. In: Winkler, Dietmar, Biffl, Stefan, Bergsmann, Johannes (eds.) SWQD 2014. LNBIP, vol. 166, pp. 185–198. Springer, Heidelberg (2014)
8. Fraser, G., Arcuri, A.: Evosuite at the SBST 2013 tool competition. In: International Workshop on Search-Based Software Testing (SBST), pp. 406–409 (2013)
9. Fraser, G., Arcuri, A.: Whole test suite generation. IEEE Trans. Software Eng. **39**(2), 276–291 (2013)
10. Fraser, G., Zeller, A.: Mutation-driven generation of unit tests and oracles. IEEE Trans. Softw. Eng. (TSE) **28**(2), 278–292 (2012)
11. Galeotti, J.P., Fraser, G., Arcuri, A.: Improving search-based test suite generation with dynamic symbolic execution. In: IEEE International Symposium on Software Reliability Engineering (ISSRE) (2013)

T3, a Combinator-Based Random Testing Tool for Java: Benchmarking

I.S. Wishnu B. Prasetya[✉]

Department of Information and Computer Sciences,
Utrecht University, Utrecht, The Netherlands
S.W.B.Prasetya@uu.nl

Abstract. T3 is the next generation of the light weight automated testing tool T2 for Java. In the heart T3 is still a random testing tool; but it now comes with some new features: pair-wise testing, concurrent generators, and a combinator-based approach ala QuickCheck. This paper presents the result of benchmarking of T3 on its default configuration against a set of real world classes.

Keywords: Automated testing java · Random testing · Benchmark testing tools

1 Introduction

T3 is the next generation of the light weight testing tool T2 [7] to automatically test Java classes; a summary is shown in Table 1. T3 is implemented in the new Java 8, and heavily exploits its new features, in particular *closures* and *streams*. T3 tests at the class level; and like its predecessor, in the heart it is a random testing tool. A typical a Java class specifies objects with a common state structure. The state of such an object is formed by a number fields, and the object has a set of public methods to query or change its state. A test-sequence against a Class Under Test (CUT) starts with the creation of an object which is an instance of the CUT, followed by calls to the object's methods, or updates to its fields. T3 randomly generates a large amount of such test sequences to trigger faulty behavior, and thus finding a bug.

Many real world classes do not actually fit into the above stereotype. For example, a class can be intended to be just a simple container of a set of static methods, e.g. as `java.lang.Math`. Another example is a class implementing a singleton design pattern: it has no public constructor. Although we can still test these two classes with sequences, it is not sensical or even possible to literally use the above way of generating sequences. Unfortunately, the predecessor T2 does not deal well with such non-stereotypical classes [2]. To handle them, T2's generator will have to be extended with variants to handle each of the special cases. Although the idea generating sequences is simple, testing a class is much more complicated than testing at the function level, e.g. as in QuickCheck [3].

T.E.J. Vos, K. Lakhotia, and S. Bauersfeld (Eds.): FITTEST 2013, LNCS 8432, pp. 101–110, 2014.
DOI: 10.1007/978-3-319-07785-7_7, ⓒ Springer International Publishing Switzerland 2014

Table 1. T3 profile

Prerequisites	
Static or dynamic	Dynamic testing at the class level
Software type	Java
Lifecycle phase	Unit testing, or any phase if it can be mapped to a class
Environment	Used as a command line tool or as a Java library
Knowledge & experience required	Java programming
Input and output of the tool: java classes (in) and trace files (out)	
Operation	
Interaction	Non-interactive; parameters are pre-specified
User guidance	Through pre-specified parameters and custom generators
Source of information	User manual
Maturity	First prototype
Technology behind the tool	Java 8's closure and multi-core programming through streams
Obtaining the tool and information: freely available, GPL3 license, no dedicted customer support	
Empirical evidence about the tool: this paper	

T2's implementation is already quite complex. Despite employing OO design patterns such as the Template Method pattern, further extending its engine with variants will spread its logic over too many satellite classes, and obscure it with increasing yo-yo antipatterns.

The new Java 8 gives us a solution. It supports *closure* —a feature which has long been requested, but only now added. It now becomes possible to program with 'higher order functions' (also known as 'combinators') as in functional programming languages. We re-implemented T2, almost from scratch. The generators are now composed with combinators, ala QuickCheck [3] in Haskell. Such an approach allows us to abstractly compose various generators. The logic of such a composition remains visible in its own code, rather than scattered in multiple classes.

To see if T3 can actually scale up to deal with real world classes, we participated in the FITTEST 2013 testing tool contest [1]. Section 3 presents a summary of the result and gives some discussion. The full result can be found in the Appendix. In Sect. 2 we first briefly give an overview of T3's new features compared to T2 [7]. In Sect. 4 we conclude.

2   T3's Features

T3's typical work cycle is as follows. Given a CUT, it generates a specified number of test sequences. Sequences that throw an exception such as an *Illegal− ArgumentException* are regarded as violating some intended pre-conditions. Such sequences are *invalid* and are dropped. Sequences throwing other kinds of exceptions, such as *NullPointerException* or *AssertionError*, are considered as revealing bugs. They are saved. Some or all of these bug sequences are later replayed for inspection by the user.

T3 can also be used to generate *clean* test sequences —this is the mode we will use in the FITTEST benchmarking. These are sequences that do not throw any exception. If the CUT is assumed to be correct, clean sequences can be saved to be used later for regression test. T3 can also inject oracles in these sequences. Let σ is a clean sequence, operating on an instance o of the CUT. Its *return value* is the value returned by the method called in σ's last step. It's *last state* is the state of o at the end of σ. These two values are used as oracles by T3: when σ is replayed for regression, it should return the same value, and yield the same last state.

At the class level, a bug can also be caused by faulty interactions between methods. Such a bug cannot be found if we just test each method individually. To make sure that T3 at least try to hunt such bugs, we apply some degree of *pair-wise testing*. For every mutator method m_1 of the CUT, and every method m_2 of the CUT, the pair (m_1, m_2) is set as a test objective: T3 will try to generate random sequences of some length (specified by the user), each containing the pair as a segment. For a CUT with many methods (some do have over a hundred!), the number of such pairs may explode. Each mutator m_1 will then be paired with k randomly selected m_2, such that the total number of pairs does not exceed a certain maximum (currently 1000). To make sure that methods and method-pairs are equally tested, sequences are generated such that every method is exercised by at least M sequences, and every method pair is exercised by at least P_M sequences. M is user-specified. P_M is calculated from M and the average occurrences of the methods in the pairs. T3 will try, but does not guarantee that such coverage is met, because in reality some test sequence may turn out to be invalid (see above) and have to be dropped. In some cases, generating enough valid sequence can indeed be very hard.

Internally, we will need various generators: one to generate a whole test suite (consisting of test sequences), several to generate different kinds of sequences, and a whole array of them for values and objects which are needed as inputs for the methods called in the sequences. In T3, generators are instances of a generic function of type $r \rightarrow v$, where r and v are type variables. Such a function takes a 'requirement' and produces an object of type v, or it fails, which is represented by the value *null*. Such a function can be defined as a traditional method, or constructed freely with a λ-expression. For example, below we specify an integer generator; the notation $r \rightarrow ...$ specifies a λ-expression in Java 8.

> $r \rightarrow$ **if** (...r specifies an integer)
>   **return new** CONST($random.nextInt(\beta - \alpha) + \alpha$) ;
>   **else return** *null* ; /* fail */

More complex generators are composed by combining simpler generators. E.g. if g is a generator the expression g.WithChance(p) constructs a new generator that behaves as p with chance p, and else fails (thus with chance $1-p$).

In functional programming, the method WithChance is also called a *combinator* [8]; note that it is a higher order function, taking another function g as a parameter, and returns a new function. Another example is FirstOf$(g_1, g_2, ...)$. It constructs a new generator, which if given a requirement r it applies its constituent generators one by one, until one succeeds on r. For example, T3's object generator is specified as below, using combinators:

> FirstOf($nullgen()$.WithChance(0.05),
> $primitives()$,
>   ...,
> $constructorgen.useConstructor()$,
> $constructorgen.useProtectedConstructor()$.WithChance(0.35),
>   /* if all the above fail, generate null: */
> $nullgen()$)

For T3's developers, combinators allow generators, including those required to handle non-stereotypical classes, to be specified more abstractly. Implementing an algorithm with combinators is more natural, leading to code which is easier to understand for future maintenance. In contrast, classical OO architecture often forces us to unnaturally defragment an algorithm over multiple classes. Visitor pattern is a prime example of that, whereas in a functional language we have a more natural tree folding to do the same.

T3 allows the user to supply his own custom object generator. Sequence and suite generators are more complex, and are thus not exposed for user extensions.

T3 generates test sequences *on the fly*. This means that the sequences are immediately executed as they are generated. In particular, there is no separate compilation phase of the test cases, as in some other tools. This makes T3 pretty fast. Its run typically only takes few seconds, which makes T3 to suit well for quick development-time testing: as the programmer is developing a class C, after each modification or refactoring he can use T3 to 'stress' C by generating a large amount of random test-sequences to trigger erroneous inter-method interactions. In such a working mode, short response time is indeed desirable; waiting for minutes would distract or annoy the programmer.

To boost its performance, T3 exploits Java 8's new stream library for parallel processing. For example, to concurrently apply a generator g on a list rs of requirements, and then reducing the results with an (associative) function $\oplus$ we simply do:

$$rs.parallelStream().map(g).reduce(unit, \oplus)$$

The *parallelStream* method essentially turns a traditional list into a 'parallel list', whose elements can be processed in parallel. Importantly, we do not need to manually program how to schedule and balance the threads on available physical cores. This is done in the background by the library. T3 uses stream to generate the sequences for each test objective (which is a pair of methods, as explained before) in parallel.

3   Benchmarking

To see if T3 can scale up to real world classes we let it participate in the
FITTEST 2013 contest for testing tools [1]. The constest set a benchmark consisting of 63 classes from 9 real world open source projects, e.g. Hibernate and
Twitter4j —see Table 2. From each project, the package that is mostly referred
to is selected. Then some classes with highest nested block depth in the package
are selected for the benchmark.

We were not allowed to know the classes upfront. So, no custom generators
can be written either. We simply run T3 with its default/base generators. This
is not how we expect a random testing tool to be used in practice. For example,
generating strings representing valid postal codes will be extremely difficult for
a random tool. So, if a CUT requires something like that as inputs, the user
has to help the tool by writing custom generators. Nevertheless, we still want to
know how T3 will perform simply by using its default generators. For each CUT,
T3 is configured to generate two test suites: S and S_{clean}. The first may contain
unclean sequences; the latter is filtered to contain only clean ones. Their sizes are
set not to exceed $6N$ and $120N$ respectively, where N is the number of methods
in the CUT. The sequences' maximum length is set to 5 and 8 respectively, for
S and S_{clean}.

There are two other tools participating in the contest, namely Randoop and
EvoSuite. The benchmark also compares the tools against manual testing. Randoop is a feedback directed random testing tool [5]. Each test sequence is built
incrementally, one test step at a time. If a test step fails, it does not drop the

Table 2. The classes in the FITTEST 2013 benchmark

Nr	Class	Project	LOC	Nr	Class	Project	LOC
1	SearchException	Hibernate	15	32	Link	GData JavaClient	190
2	Version	Hibernate	12	33	OtherContent	GData JavaClient	179
3	BackendFactory	Hibernate	72	34	OutOfLineContent	GData JavaClient	102
4	FlushLuceneWork	Hibernate	26	35	Source	GData JavaClient	324
5	OptimizeLuceneWork	Hibernate	26	36	CharMatcher	Guava	824
6	LoggerFactory	Hibernate	14	37	Joiner	Guava	222
7	LoggerHelper	Hibernate	17	38	Objects	Guava	130
8	OAuthConfig	Scribe	63	39	Predicates	Guava	379
9	OAuthRequest	Scribe	36	40	SmallCharMatcher	Guava	92
10	ParameterList	Scribe	95	41	Splitter	Guava	266
11	Request	Scribe	213	42	Suppliers	Guava	172
12	Response	Scribe	72	43	CategoryDescendantsIterator	JWPL	103
13	Token	Scribe	64	44	CycleHandler	JWPL	71
14	Verifier	Scribe	15	45	Page	JWPL	351
15	ExceptionDiagnosis	Twitter4j	73	46	PageIterator	JWPL	182
16	GeoQuery	Twitter4j	126	47	PageQueryIterable	JWPL	131
17	OEmbedRequest	Twitter4j	147	48	Title	JWPL	79
18	Paging	Twitter4j	171	49	WikipediaInfo	JWPL	222
19	TwitterBaseImpl	Twitter4j	328	50	AbstractLoader	eclipse-cs	77
20	TwitterException	Twitter4j	237	51	AnnotationUtility	eclipse-cs	78
21	TwitterImpl	Twitter4j	1187	52	AutomaticBean	eclipse-cs	178
22	AsyncHttpClient	Async HttpClient	296	53	FileContents	eclipse-cs	161
23	AsyncHttpClientConfig	Async HttpClient	621	54	FileText	eclipse-cs	184
24	FluentCaseInsensitive-StringsMap	Async HttpClient	292	55	ScopeUtils	eclipse-cs	189
25	FluentStringsMap	Async HttpClient	240	56	Utils	eclipse-cs	160
26	Realm	Async HttpClient	481	57	AbstractInstance	JMLL	136
27	RequestBuilderBase	Async HttpClient	544	58	Complex	JMLL	53
28	SimpleAsyncHttpClient	Async HttpClient	610	59	DefaultDataset	JMLL	152
29	AttributeHelper	GData JavaClient	344	60	DenseInstance	JMLL	155
30	DateTime	GData JavaClient	264	61	Fold	JMLL	201
31	Kind	GData JavaClient	189	62	SparseInstance	JMLL	191
				63	ARFFHandler	JMLL	51

Table 3. Results

	Manual	Randoop	EvoSuite	T3
average cov_i	67.78 %	31.58 %	58.27 %	44.81 %
average cov_b	50.90 %	19.02 %	47.34 %	26.68 %
average cov_m	50.21 %	20.39 %	42.58 %	33.38 %
average t_{gen}	21.83 m	1.68 m	3.83 m	31.32 s
average t_{exec}	0.01 m	1.61 s	5.04 s	24.96 s
Score	210.45	93.45	199.57	144.98

entire sequence and starts over. Instead, it tries to regenerate the step. T3 actually also does the same (which was called 'search-mode' in T2). EvoSuite is based on a genetic algorithm [4].

The results are summarized in Table 3; the full results can be found in Table 4 in the Appendix. All tools are run on the same machine: an Intel(R) Core(TM)2 Quad CPU Q9550, 2.83 GHz with 8 GB main memory, running Ubuntu 12.04. 1 LTS. T3 does not crash on any of the given classes, which we take as a good indicator for its robustness. Table 3 shows the average instruction, branch, and mutation coverage (cov_i, cov_b, and cov_m) achieved by each tool over the whole benchmark suite. Generation-time, t_{gen}, is the time used by a tool to generate a suite. Execution-time, t_{exec} is the suite's execution time. 'Score' is some weighted summation of the other metrics, see [1].

3.1 Discussion

For measuring instruction and branch coverage, the benchmark counts both clean and unclean test cases. For mutation test, the classes in the benchmark are assumed to be correct, and the tools must generate clean test cases as well, when possible with oracles. Mutation test is then used to see how well these clean suite can find artificially inserted bugs. That is why T3 generates S and S_{clean}.

Unfortunately, the use of mutation test forced T3 to do its work in two stages, rather than purely on-the-fly: the generated test suite has to be saved in a file, to be later replayed during a separate mutation test phase. Since the suite was already executed when it was generated, its effective t_{exec} is actually 0, rather than the number reported by the benchmark.

Some of the target classes seem to contain non-determinism. During the generation-phase we double check that S_{clean} is indeed clean, but during the replay some sequences may still turn out to throw exceptions. The used mutation tool unfortunately reacts by disqualifying the entire suite! To work around this, we split S_{clean} into up to 100 smaller suites, each containing at least 10 sequences. This however, significantly increases T3's t_{gen}, due to increased IO operations. Its normal t_{gen} should thus be smaller than indicated in Table 3.

Whereas in a previous contest [6] the predecessor T2 was outperformed by Randoop, the new implementation T3 now outperforms Randoop. These tools share the same 'feed-back directed random sequence generation', as it is called in

Randoop [5], but T3 is significantly faster, while delivering higher coverage. T3's much larger t_{exec} suggests that it generates much larger suite, and this could be the reason why its coverage is better than Randoop. Both random testing tools cannot beat EvoSuite's genetic algorithm. Only later (and too late) we realized that T3's way of producing clean suites is as such that it will only produce clean *positive* test sequences. For example, if a call $m(0)$ in a test sequence σ throws an *IllegalArgumentException*, T3 will drop σ from S_{clean}. However, in this benchmark m is assumed to be correct. So, testing that $m(0)$ indeed throws an *IllegalArgumentException* is actually a valid way of testing m; but notice that it is a *negative* test. This could have easily been programmed in T3, but as it was, T3 forgot to produce negative tests; whereas EvoSuite can generate them. This may explain T3's lower branch coverage compared to EvoSuite.

There are 21 classes on which T3 performs very badly ($\leq 5\%$ cov_b). Seven of them turns out to be classes with no branches, so we are left with 14 actual problematic classes. Most of them turn out to be hard classes to test, even for human: manual testing's average cov_b over them is 30.6%, compared to its 44.8% average over the entire benchmark suite. Ten of these classes are hard for all three tools (they perform just as bad).

This leaves only four classes which are specifically problematic for T3: *DefaultDataset*, *AttributeHelper*, *Kind*, and *Suppliers*. It turns out that the problems are more engineering in nature, or incompleteness in the range of non-stereotypical classes that T3 is programmed to handle. *DefaultDataset* turns out to be extending *ArrayList*, which has a different set of methods in Java 8 and Java 7. T3 has to be run in Java 8. However, the benchmark tools requires test suites to be run in Java 7. This causes all suites of *DefaultDataset* to fail to load, and so T3 gets 0 coverage.

AttributeHelper has a single constructor that expects a parameter of type *Attributes*. This type is actually an interface, so it cannot be directly instantiated. We need to have at least one concrete class that implements it. T3 is configured to search the CUT's *src* directory for possible implementations of interfaces. We do not let T3 to scan the entire class paths of the benchmark (which is very long), as this seems rather wasteful. In practice, the user can be expected to give sufficient class paths to T3.

A large part, or even the whole part, of *Kind* and *Suppliers* consists of inner classes. Currently T3 simply does not cover them.

There are five classes where T3 performs quite well ($\geq 70\%$ cov_b), shown in the table below, and compared with EvoSuite and manual testing.

		cov_b in %		
	LOC	T3	EvoSuite	Manual
8 OAuthConfig	63	75	100	100
24 FluentCaseInsensitiveStringsMap	292	86.79	67.25	50.94
25 FluentStringsMap	240	84.55	67.11	46.51
56 Utils	160	71.43	78.02	92.31
57 AbstractInstance	136	70.41	67.86	92.86

For some of the above classes, we can see that manual testing is still significantly better; though on the other hand the human testers take in average 20.61 min to write their test cases for the above classes (t_{gen}), whereas T3 does it in about 12 s; EvoSuite's average is 3.41 min.

In two cases, *FluentCaseInsensitiveStringsMap* and *FluentStringsMap*, T3 even manages to beat manual testing. Many methods in these two classes take parameters containing bounded type variables, e.g.:

public void *putAll*(*Map*⟨? **extends** *String*, ? **extends** *List*⟨*String*⟩⟩ *values*) {...}

Obviously we cannot just give any instance of *Map* to *putAll*; it has to be of a specific type as specified above. It could that human testers find it more difficult to handle methods like that; and it seems that EvoSuite needs more effort than T3 as well. One of the improvement T3 adds with respect to T2, is a more powerful way to deal with type variables. For the above case, it will be able to infer a right concrete type to be used for *values*. However, the type system of Java, in particular when type variables are involved, is also quite complex. T3 only partially covers it; and it is still on-going work to improve it.

4   Conclusion and Future Work

The result does not directly tell us if T3 improves T2, but it does outperform Randoop whereas previously T2 was outperformed by Randoop [2]. Admittedly, the latter was measured on a different benchmark [2]. We did try to run T3 on at least a subset of [2] and it does perform much better than T2. The improvement comes mainly from better handling of non-stereotypical classes. The new combinator-based architecture helps a lot in implementing this.

On average, T3 cannot beat EvoSuite's genetic algorithm; the difference is quite significant. The under-performance can partly be explained by e.g. its negligence to generate negative tests, technological problems, or incompleteness in implementation (Subsect. 3.1), but it is unclear in how much these factors influence the result. Our guess is that simply including negative tests will give T3 significant boost. Another point to note is that EvoSuite instruments the CUT, and T3 does not, leading to the question: how close a random-based tool like T3 can get to EvoSuite if it also does instrumentation? While still relying on brute force, this would enable T3 to better spread its effort over the branches in the CUT. However, the challenge is to keep the overall run time short, which is crucial for usage in short-cycles development-time testing. Although T3 is already the fastest of the three, the average generation-time of 30 s should be shorter. This is future work.

Dealing with Java type variables also seem to be a hurdle for automated testing tools. A better way to handle Java's complex type system is required, to be able to properly instantiate parameters. T3 has made an attempt towards this, with limited success. However, its treatment is still incomplete. This too, is future work.

Furthermore, with the coming Java 8, the testing tools will have to deal with higher order functions/methods. Such methods take functions as parameters, which are much more challenging to generate than plain objects.

A   Appendix: FITTEST 2013 Contest's Full Results

Table 4. FITTEST 2013 contest's full results

Variable (values are averaged over 7 runs, times are in minutes (if not otherwise specified), coverage is in percent)

Class	Manual t_{gen}	t_{exec}	cov_i	cov_b	cov_m	Randoop t_{gen}	t_{exec}	cov_i	cov_b	cov_m	EvoSuite t_{gen}	t_{exec}	cov_i	cov_b	cov_m	T3 t_{gen}	t_{exec}	cov_i	cov_b	cov_m
	$t_{prep}=0.00$ min					$t_{prep}=0.00$ min					$t_{prep}=0.00$ min					$t_{prep}=0.00$ min				
1	2.58	0.01	100.00	0.00	0.00	1.68	0.02	100.00	0.00	0.00	3.23	0.00	0.00	0.00	0.00	0.24	0.66	100.00	0.00	0.00
2	2.00	0.01	100.00	0.00	100.00	1.67	0.01	100.00	0.00	0.00	3.74	0.01	60.00	0.00	0.00	0.03	0.16	70.00	0.00	0.00
3	52.12	0.01	100.00	93.75	93.33	1.67	0.01	2.26	0.00	0.00	4.53	0.02	27.71	6.25	40.95	0.09	0.11	27.82	6.25	33.33
4	10.93	0.01	100.00	100.00	100.00	1.67	0.01	0.00	0.00	0.00	3.22	0.03	89.74	100.00	75.00	0.12	0.53	61.54	50.00	50.00
5	5.33	0.01	100.00	100.00	100.00	1.67	0.00	0.00	0.00	0.00	3.22	0.03	89.74	100.00	75.00	0.13	0.53	61.54	50.00	50.00
6	5.20	0.01	90.63	0.00	100.00	1.67	0.01	56.25	0.00	50.00	7.75	0.01	17.41	0.00	0.00	0.09	0.06	46.88	0.00	50.00
7	5.27	0.01	100.00	0.00	33.33	1.67	0.01	70.83	0.00	33.33	3.73	0.01	87.50	0.00	33.33	0.03	0.16	58.33	0.00	33.33
8	15.00	0.01	91.14	100.00	100.00	1.71	0.19	68.35	50.00	88.89	3.21	0.05	91.14	100.00	100.00	0.04	0.30	70.89	75.00	88.89
9	20.00	0.01	100.00	100.00	80.00	1.67	0.00	0.00	0.00	0.00	3.15	0.03	100.00	100.00	80.00	0.21	0.72	44.44	0.00	40.00
10	30.00	0.01	96.71	88.89	82.61	1.69	0.03	84.51	83.33	86.96	3.19	0.06	99.60	96.83	81.99	0.04	0.37	97.65	88.89	90.06
11	21.00	0.01	73.40	54.55	37.21	1.67	0.00	0.00	0.00	0.00	3.19	0.11	64.45	40.91	37.21	0.19	0.67	47.61	31.82	39.53
12	18.00	0.01	94.69	60.00	82.35	1.67	0.00	0.00	0.00	0.00	3.14	0.01	1.77	0.00	0.00	0.30	0.01	0.00	0.00	0.00
13	13.00	0.01	100.00	87.50	86.36	1.71	0.15	89.92	87.50	72.73	3.17	0.08	100.00	94.64	90.91	0.03	0.33	76.47	43.75	63.64
14	17.00	0.01	100.00	0.00	100.00	1.68	0.01	100.00	0.00	50.00	3.13	0.01	100.00	0.00	50.00	0.02	0.07	100.00	0.00	50.00
15	22.00	0.01	52.42	66.67	40.00	1.67	0.00	0.00	0.00	0.00	3.27	0.07	98.30	91.27	60.00	0.05	0.33	79.30	61.11	45.71
16	20.00	0.01	43.62	45.83	50.79	1.69	0.05	49.73	47.92	52.38	3.30	0.18	100.00	95.83	81.86	0.05	0.59	80.32	41.67	68.25
17	10.00	0.01	53.05	46.30	33.78	1.68	0.01	49.05	35.19	25.68	3.30	0.17	95.47	88.36	57.14	0.08	0.64	81.49	48.15	61.78
18	22.00	0.01	49.42	52.78	41.33	1.69	0.06	56.59	52.78	49.33	3.24	0.14	93.91	91.27	68.76	0.09	0.62	82.17	58.33	76.00
19	17.00	0.03	27.96	24.51	22.86	1.67	0.00	0.00	0.00	0.00	6.73	0.04	9.16	6.16	3.54	0.02	0.00	0.00	0.00	0.00
20	30.00	0.01	53.11	44.90	54.22	1.69	0.03	59.52	41.84	55.42	3.40	0.24	78.15	70.12	17.56	0.19	0.65	59.59	33.67	36.83
21	15.00	0.15	4.07	12.50	1.08	1.67	0.00	0.00	0.00	0.00	2.75	0.06	1.11	3.90	0.36	6.01	0.00	0.00	0.00	0.00
22	20.00	0.02	44.47	35.71	41.54	1.69	0.07	39.86	25.00	0.00	9.02	0.00	0.00	0.00	0.00	0.22	1.05	49.54	27.38	21.54
23	20.00	0.01	78.92	43.33	19.09	1.67	0.00	0.00	0.00	0.00	8.71	0.11	39.76	27.62	32.34	0.03	0.00	0.00	0.00	0.00
24	10.00	0.01	56.33	50.94	44.44	1.68	0.01	88.60	65.63	73.59	3.35	0.24	74.62	67.25	68.69	0.09	0.71	89.47	86.79	87.59
25	15.00	0.01	53.82	46.51	39.53	1.69	0.01	86.68	63.95	73.26	3.11	0.24	72.77	67.11	65.95	0.09	0.71	87.11	84.55	86.05
26	30.00	0.01	81.81	41.53	54.24	1.67	0.00	0.00	0.00	0.00	3.43	0.28	92.98	64.65	70.09	0.13	0.70	31.48	21.19	29.17
27	13.00	0.01	38.78	24.59	23.93	1.67	0.00	0.00	0.00	0.00	8.59	0.09	23.76	21.31	16.83	0.02	0.00	0.00	0.00	0.00
28	19.00	0.02	29.68	29.51	15.65	1.68	0.00	0.00	0.00	0.00	2.70	0.00	0.00	0.00	0.00	9.35	0.01	4.24	4.22	1.69
29	25.00	0.01	30.92	31.71	37.50	1.67	0.00	0.00	0.00	0.00	3.45	0.22	85.90	80.49	59.07	2.59	0.01	0.00	0.00	0.00
30	20.00	0.01	52.43	40.00	43.69	1.71	0.21	92.48	77.14	0.14	3.30	0.19	78.97	67.55	56.59	0.07	0.59	51.16	31.43	50.49
31	16.00	0.01	39.95	34.09	28.26	1.67	0.01	5.21	0.00	0.00	3.36	0.06	55.31	43.83	46.27	0.07	0.08	3.62	0.00	2.17
32	13.00	0.01	39.41	41.89	20.00	1.69	0.03	21.19	9.46	26.67	3.79	0.17	62.98	59.46	36.43	0.35	1.23	57.25	45.75	34.76
33	10.00	0.01	12.66	11.36	15.00	1.69	0.05	16.89	9.09	27.50	4.37	0.09	46.85	37.01	36.07	0.08	0.80	56.99	50.00	47.50
34	9.00	0.01	25.97	25.00	16.67	1.71	0.18	15.58	0.00	25.00	4.13	0.15	83.55	81.12	67.26	0.08	0.63	62.34	42.86	41.67
35	20.00	0.01	22.43	22.73	19.13	1.69	0.02	27.24	15.91	23.48	3.47	0.23	42.59	30.84	33.04	0.38	1.23	46.45	37.01	43.73
36	17.00	0.01	63.21	57.07	48.60	1.67	0.00	0.00	0.00	0.00	6.96	0.07	70.86	65.00	47.73	0.31	0.06	20.47	7.33	5.03
37	15.00	0.01	61.80	65.22	46.81	1.69	0.02	60.52	60.87	57.45	3.30	0.09	84.40	90.06	77.20	0.20	0.69	49.14	34.78	0.00
38	11.00	0.01	60.30	61.11	45.95	1.68	0.01	30.34	38.89	24.32	3.24	0.12	96.20	79.37	96.14	0.08	0.17	32.10	43.65	29.34
39	30.00	0.01	37.40	27.08	25.66	1.69	0.01	29.09	6.25	10.62	3.31	0.13	36.99	19.35	22.63	0.18	0.60	34.42	6.33	16.81
40	12.00	0.01	63.46	46.15	20.83	1.67	0.00	0.00	0.00	0.00	3.22	0.02	25.77	30.77	26.79	0.07	0.19	39.42	19.23	22.32
41	17.00	0.01	84.86	73.08	67.03	1.69	0.02	79.04	77.11	59.34	3.24	0.11	93.74	87.91	82.89	0.12	0.63	40.49	7.97	20.88
42	9.00	0.01	78.01	54.17	59.09	1.69	0.01	21.99	8.33	11.80	3.18	0.04	30.03	21.43	27.60	0.08	0.07	8.90	0.00	6.82
43	10.00	0.01	89.25	66.67	65.38	1.67	0.00	0.00	0.00	0.00	2.52	0.00	0.00	0.00	0.00	0.37	0.01	0.00	0.00	0.00
44	45.00	0.01	91.33	77.14	69.75	1.67	0.00	0.00	0.00	0.00	2.84	0.00	0.00	0.00	0.00	0.09	0.05	14.80	14.29	3.36
45	20.00	0.03	0.00	0.00	0.00	1.67	0.00	0.00	0.00	0.00	3.03	0.00	0.00	0.00	0.00	0.48	0.01	0.00	0.00	0.00
46	26.00	0.01	49.01	42.86	45.83	1.67	0.00	0.00	0.00	0.00	2.84	0.00	0.00	0.00	0.00	0.08	0.34	46.04	36.05	36.31
47	20.00	0.01	45.36	18.60	2.22	1.67	0.00	0.00	0.00	0.00	2.95	0.00	0.00	0.00	0.00	0.08	0.01	0.00	0.00	0.00
48	10.00	0.01	89.51	87.50	50.00	1.72	0.18	58.64	62.50	85.71	3.17	0.03	76.01	76.79	92.86	0.03	0.49	57.41	50.00	50.00
49	35.00	0.01	24.93	18.00	20.90	1.67	0.00	0.00	0.00	0.00	3.44	0.00	0.00	0.00	0.00	6.01	0.00	0.00	0.00	0.00
50	21.68	0.01	62.00	25.00	30.00	1.67	0.00	0.00	0.00	0.00	3.30	0.01	77.00	50.00	18.57	0.04	0.00	0.00	0.00	0.00
51	74.13	0.01	88.44	86.67	100.00	1.67	0.00	0.00	0.00	0.00	3.24	0.10	58.11	54.29	46.75	0.05	0.08	20.41	16.67	18.18
52	38.72	0.01	55.24	57.14	20.93	1.67	0.01	0.53	0.00	0.00	4.45	0.02	49.45	29.59	13.29	0.09	0.32	44.76	21.43	13.95
53	31.87	0.01	76.88	38.46	42.00	1.70	0.10	82.17	61.54	66.00	3.35	0.10	59.57	53.30	50.29	0.09	0.71	71.71	53.30	54.86
54	47.68	0.01	81.60	73.08	61.70	1.67	0.00	0.00	0.00	0.00	3.43	0.09	48.53	45.00	55.93	0.54	0.08	17.60	11.54	10.64
55	58.35	0.01	77.22	51.00	60.66	1.67	0.00	0.00	0.00	0.00	4.73	0.05	48.73	33.29	10.07	0.03	0.35	25.63	11.00	29.51
56	42.32	0.01	96.36	92.31	90.48	1.68	0.01	54.25	61.54	61.90	3.49	0.13	55.75	78.02	65.31	0.04	0.50	74.73	71.43	68.03
57	20.73	0.01	97.02	92.86	65.63	1.67	0.00	0.00	0.00	0.00	3.69	0.08	87.06	67.86	68.08	0.74	1.22	86.67	70.41	71.88
58	26.17	0.01	100.00	0.00	74.19	1.68	0.01	100.00	0.00	93.55	3.18	0.08	100.00	0.00	47.93	0.04	0.53	100.00	0.00	100.00
59	28.40	0.01	95.76	90.00	53.23	1.69	0.00	0.00	0.00	0.00	3.30	0.10	95.04	97.14	60.60	0.16	0.55	0.00	0.00	0.00
60	24.77	0.01	87.50	87.50	67.74	1.69	0.02	94.57	87.50	0.00	4.07	0.15	98.84	98.66	76.73	0.76	1.31	84.08	56.25	67.74
61	17.20	0.01	86.39	80.00	56.25	1.67	0.00	0.00	0.00	0.00	3.26	0.16	87.56	82.86	80.36	0.22	0.74	39.99	40.00	59.38
62	53.58	0.01	91.86	81.25	64.71	1.69	0.02	94.88	75.00	0.00	3.32	0.16	98.17	87.50	72.90	0.34	1.10	91.86	62.50	77.52
63	9.00	0.01	97.46	100.00	50.00	1.67	0.01	2.54	0.00	0.00	3.15	0.01	0.00	0.00	0.00	0.03	0.09	36.44	25.00	16.67

	Manual	Randoop	EvoSuite	T3
Files	63.00	207.43	777.43	3385.71
Instructions	16006.86 / 32917 (48.63%)	6821.86 / 32917 (20.72%)	15115.43 / 32917 (45.92%)	9830.71 / 32917 (29.87%)
Branches	1145.00 / 2555 (44.81%)	494.57 / 2555 (19.36%)	1219.14 / 2555 (47.72%)	653.43 / 2555 (25.57%)
Mutants	1499.00 / 3903 (38.41%)	585.00 / 3903 (14.99%)	1524.86 / 3903 (39.07%)	1041.43 / 3903 (26.68%)
CB Mutations	71.14 / 195 (36.48%)	20.00 / 195 (10.26%)	80.71 / 195 (41.39%)	47.00 / 195 (24.10%)
NC Mutations	572.86 / 1252 (45.76%)	198.00 / 1252 (15.81%)	510.71 / 1252 (40.79%)	322.86 / 1252 (25.79%)
M Mutations	120.00 / 334 (35.93%)	40.00 / 334 (11.98%)	144.00 / 334 (43.11%)	131.71 / 334 (39.43%)
I Mutations	69.00 / 101 (68.32%)	7.00 / 101 (6.93%)	64.86 / 101 (64.21%)	23.14 / 101 (22.91%)
IN Mutations	3.00 / 6 (50.00%)	1.00 / 6 (16.67%)	1.71 / 6 (28.57%)	2.00 / 6 (33.33%)
RV Mutations	605.86 / 1576 (38.44%)	294.00 / 1576 (18.65%)	647.86 / 1576 (41.11%)	430.71 / 1576 (27.33%)
VMC Mutations	57.14 / 439 (13.02%)	25.00 / 439 (5.69%)	75.00 / 439 (17.08%)	84.00 / 439 (19.13%)
Avg. cov_i	67.78%	31.58%	58.27%	44.81%
Avg. cov_b	50.90%	19.02%	47.34%	26.68%
Avg. cov_m	50.21%	20.39%	42.58%	33.38%
Avg. t_{gen}	21.83 m	1.68 m	3.83 m	31.32 s
Avg. t_{exec}	0.01 m	1.61 s	5.04 s	24.96 s
Total t_{gen}	22.92 h	1.77 h	4.02 h	32.88 m
Total t_{exec}	0.72 m	1.69 m	5.29 m	26.20 m
Score	210.45	93.45	199.57	144.98

References

1. Bauersfeld, S., Vos, T., Lakhotia, K.: Unit testing tool competition - round two. In: Workshop on Future Internet Testing (FITTEST) (2013)
2. Bauersfeld, S., Vos, T., Lakhotia, K., Poulding, S., Condori, N.: Unit testing tool competition. In: International Workshop on Search-Based Software Testing (SBST) (2013)
3. Claessen, K., Hughes, J.: QuickCheck: a lightweight tool for random testing of Haskell programs. In: ACM International Conference on Functional Programming (ICFP) (2000)
4. Fraser, G., Arcuri, A.: Evosuite: automatic test suite generation for object-oriented software. In: SIGSOFT FSE, pp. 416–419 (2011)
5. Pacheco, C., Ernst, M.D.: Randoop: feedback-directed random testing for Java. In: Companion to the 22nd ACM SIGPLAN Conference on Object-Oriented Programming Systems and Applications (OOPSLA), pp. 815–816. ACM (2007)
6. Prasetya, I.: Measuring T2 against SBST 2013 benchmark suite. In: Proceedings of 6th International Conference on Software Testing, Verification and Validation Workshops (ICSTW) (2013)
7. Prasetya, I., Vos, T., Baars, A.: Trace-based reflexive testing of OO programs with T2. In: 1st Interenational Conference on Software Testing, Verification, and Validation (ICST) (2008)
8. Swierstra, S.: Combinator parsers: from toys to tools. Electron. Notes Theoret. Comput. Sci. **41**(1), 38–59 (2001)

Author Index

Printed in the United States
By Bookmasters